PRECIOUS METAL

In memory of

Squadron Leader Nicholas Cree
Flight Lieutenant Hayden Madsen
Flying Officer Daniel Gregory
Corporal Benjamin Carson

Ake Ake Kia Kaha

PRECIOUS METAL

CLASSIC FIGHTERS IN NEW ZEALAND

GAVIN CONROY

craig potton publishing

First published in 2011 by Craig Potton Publishing
98 Vickerman Street, PO Box 555, Nelson, New Zealand
www.craigpotton.co.nz

© Craig Potton Publishing
© Gavin Conroy
Cover design by Chris Chisnall

ISBN 978 1 877517 35 8

Printed in China by Midas Printing International Ltd

CONTENTS

FOREWORD
Keith Skilling

The first solo flight in a WWII fighter is a very memorable experience for any pilot. The adrenalin rush, smell, power and torque, unfamiliar controls and inputs, the cost of getting there and the underlying thoughts of historic value and 'don't bend it', all add up to a pretty heady combination. It wasn't quite like that for me.

After more than twenty years of flying the Harvard I got a phone call from Tim Wallis one evening. Phone calls from Tim are either very short, or very long and always very interesting. This one was short.

'Hi Keith, I've just bought a Corsair, it's in Texas and I would like you to pick it up and fly it to Longbeach where we will put it on a ship and bring it back to New Zealand.'

'Hey Tim, that's fantastic', I replied.

'Thanks Keith, goodbye', said Tim.

I immediately set about finding out everything I could about flying a Corsair. At the time I was a First Officer on the B747 and during trips to Los Angeles and London I visited Steve Hinton at Chino, and Mark Hanna at Duxford, gaining very valuable information. Several months later, along with Ray Mulqueen, Tim's Operations Manager and Chief Engineer, I arrived at Breckenridge, Texas where the Corsair was under the care of Howard Pardue. Howard is a very well known and highly respected Corsair, (and Bearcat, Hellcat, Wildcat) pilot in the US.

'I don't like airline pilots', was his greeting in a slow Texan drawl, along with various other professions he named, 'because they break good warbirds'. We had four days for me to get checked out and do the ten hours flying required before I could ferry it to Longbeach. For the first two days Howard virtually ignored me and made no effort to start my conversion. During this period I became very acquainted with the aeroplane, sitting in it, starting it, taxiing it, wings up, wings down, shutting it

down and then cleaning it, time after time until I was becoming thoroughly bored. Ray was getting concerned and had a word with Howard about the time constraints. Howard finally relented and after a pretty tough technical question and answer session said, 'I think we can do business'. We did some flying together in his Harvard and Beech Staggerwing, and he finally announced that I was ready for my first solo in the Corsair.

I have never been more prepared for a first solo, and almost felt that I had already done it – maybe that was Howard's plan all along! So it was sadly a bit of a non-event. I just got airborne, did some stalling, played with the undercarriage, flaps etc and then did some aeros. I do remember thinking what a beautiful aircraft this was, exactly as I had expected, but I was still a bit miffed at being labelled 'only an airline pilot'. So I did exactly what any 'airline pilot' would have done, and finished the flight with a couple of very low passes over Howard. Thus, I started a long association with this magnificent aeroplane. Howard was thrilled and labelled me a real Corsair pilot, giving me one of his precious Vought badges. We have remained very good friends ever since.

A few days later the flight to Longbeach was equally interesting, but that is another story! For every aircraft and pilot mentioned in this book there are dozens of similar stories, more so for the individual aircraft because they are truly a living history. We very are fortunate in New Zealand to have people with the foresight and means to keep a large collection of these very historical aircraft flying. They are very nice to see in a museum but the sight and sound of them in the air brings real meaning to the word 'history'. Sadly, one day they will probably have to remain on the ground, but in the meantime people like Gavin Conroy have captured them in their natural environment for all time.

INTRODUCTION
Gavin Conroy

It is a great privilege to be able to present this book of historic and legendary former military aircraft from World War II. The planes featured in this book are all lovingly restored examples of aircraft that flew over Europe in the so-called 'theatres of war'. Today there are many thousands the world over who are passionate restorers and fliers of these warbirds, and it's been my pleasure to have flown beside them and captured them in photographs.

My own journey with aircraft began when I started flying at the age of sixteen, and over the next few years enjoyed flying around the countryside, taking friends and family for flights in aircraft such as the trusty Piper Tomahawk.

In around 2004 I was looking through magazines and really enjoyed the marvellous air-to-air photographs. As I had ruled out the possibility of flying a World War II fighter myself I decided that if I couldn't fly these aircraft types I could always try and fly with them.

That year, I took some ground-based photographs during the biennial Warbirds Over Wanaka festival – the hugely popular and now world-famous air show held in Wanaka that attracts tens of thousands of visitors. Afterwards Graham Orphan – editor of *Classic Wings* magazine – mentioned that he thought some of my photos from the show were pretty good and suggested I consider taking photography seriously. And so, after working through different types of cameras and learning a lot along the way, I decided to try my hand at air-to-air photography.

As a licensed pilot I had a good idea of the challenges involved: both the platform aircraft and the target aircraft are often flying at low levels while under moderate to high g-force; there are only certain times of the day that it can be done; and it can be very uncomfortable for the photographer.

On my first trial run, we removed a perfectly good door off a Piper Cherokee and took off to photograph a pair of Nanchang trainers – aircraft designed and built in China for the People's Liberation Army.

It took around twenty minutes just to get used to the fact that the door was missing, and it was cold and windy, but alongside were two aircraft being flown in perfect formation by Steve Petersen and Jay McIntyre. Upon seeing them, all of the fears and trepidation vanished and I focused on the aircraft.

That initial flight engendered a desire to pursue air-to-air photography seriously, and I began to think of the great possibilities it would offer; I also thought about a few rules to follow to ensure the flying was safe and, more importantly, the great photos we could create.

The next task was to find someone who would let me fly with their World War II fighter aeroplane. I approached Graham Bethell, who owns and flies a North American P–51D Mustang. I hadn't taken many air-to-air photos up to this point – and Graham knew that – but he agreed to fly alongside for a few minutes. Seeing a Mustang flying in close formation was spine-tingling and I probably spent the first minutes or so just admiring the view. Following the flight I was convinced that I could work in the demanding environment of air-to-air photography, and several years later it is a great thrill to flick through the pages of this book and see so many different historic aircraft that have flown in New Zealand skies.

We have flown all over New Zealand to take the photos featured in the following pages. There have been trips to Wanaka, Ohakea, Masterton, Christchurch, and sometimes to Auckland to fly with some of the World War II fighters that have been restored there.

This book is a culmination of six years work, with more than thirty-five flights and around twenty hours spent in the air. The flights often take months of planning and

at times we have flown with the subject aircraft several times, so a lot of work goes on behind the scenes to produce these images.

The book focuses on the World War II-era fighter aircraft that I have air-to-air photographs of, and features a few types that were restored here in New Zealand for overseas owners. Much sweat, tears and many painstaking hours were spent restoring these aircraft, and I felt it was very important to highlight them and the people who lovingly worked on them.

The keen eye will also note that one of the fighters we include, the Lavochkin La–9, didn't actually fly during World War II, but was designed during 1945. The La–9 was successor to the very capable Lavochkin La–5 and La–7 series of fighters, and was restored to flying condition in New Zealand. As it is the only one of its type flying in the world we have included it in *Precious Metal*.

There are many people to thank for getting this book to fruition. Dave MacDonald has put in a lot of time working on the text, as have the pilots and owners involved. Special thanks go to Craig Potton Publishing, especially Robbie Burton, for giving me a go in the first place. This book is a result of a huge team effort.

Special thanks also to all owners, pilots, engineers, and restoration teams – your work and dedication has made this book possible.

And I must also thank my ever-patient wife Jacquie. Her loyalty and support of my photography ambitions have been admirable and have sometimes meant a lot of time waiting for me to get flights completed, not to mention all the days and weekends away as well as the countless hours I have spent working on the computer.

I hope you enjoy this book as much as I have enjoyed the adventure of getting it to you.

HAWKER
HURRICANE Mk IIa
ZK–TPK (P3351)

The Hurricane is generally considered the 'workhorse' of the British Royal Air Force (RAF) in aerial combat, and was the unsung hero of the Battle of Britain in 1940. It's essentially a combination of two genres of aircraft design – the biplane and monoplane.

Designed by English aeronautical engineer Sydney Camm, work started on the fighter in 1934 following an Air Ministry request. Using many existing tools and jigs that had been used to produce the successful Hawker Fury biplanes, the aircraft was essentially a Fury monoplane and much of the structure was tube, wood and fabric.

The first prototype took to the air in November 1935 and, although faster and more advanced than the biplane fighters being used by the RAF on the front line at the time, the Hurricane's design was already outdated when introduced. Nevertheless there were some advantages to its construction: any damage was easier to repair as specialist equipment was not required, and 'assembly in the field' was much more straightforward. Bullet damage was also less likely than that of an all-metal aircraft, as ammunition was likely to pass through the airframe without exploding.

One concern, however, was the threat of fire from this type of 'combustible' construction. Metal-skinned wings gradually replaced the fabric covered examples from April 1939; the advantage of the heavier wing structure being that they allowed the carrying of bombs and rockets for its later role as a 'Hurribomber'.

By the outbreak of World War II, nearly 500 Hurricanes had been produced, and had equipped eighteen aircraft squadrons. With their steady gun platform and inferior performance to the 'thoroughbred' Spitfire and the Messerschmitt Bf 109E, Hurricanes concentrated on the Luftwaffe's bombers and claimed more than half of the RAF's kills during the Battle of Britain.

Following the battle the fighter saw some nocturnal service during the Blitz and then over occupied Europe.

Hurricanes later served with several squadrons in the Desert Air Force further afield, mainly in the ground attack and anti-tank role, and also as a fighter in the Far East.

A major operator of the type was the Soviet Union and it was from here that the featured aircraft – P3351/DR393 – was recovered from a crash site in 1991. It is a Mk IIa version of the Hurricane, which had come into service in September 1940. This particular aircraft served in the Battles of France and Britain before being shipped to the USSR where it was re-equipped with Russian cannons and was eventually shot down in 1943. The wreck was bought by New Zealand aviation entrepreneur and founder of Warbirds Over Wanaka, Sir Tim Wallis, in 1992 and rebuilt to fly at Hawker Restorations in the UK and Air New Zealand Engineering Services. Taking to the air for the first time in January 2000, the fighter made its public debut at Warbirds Over Wanaka that Easter and has flown at several Wanaka shows since.

Only twelve Hurricanes remain airworthy worldwide and it has been a pleasure to watch one of the few fly in New Zealand skies.

The Hurricane was a very successful fighter aircraft during the Battle of Britain, and shot down more enemy aircraft than the Spitfire. At the time, more Hurricanes were available and many squadrons were tasked with shooting down bombers while the Spitfires attacked the fighter escorts.

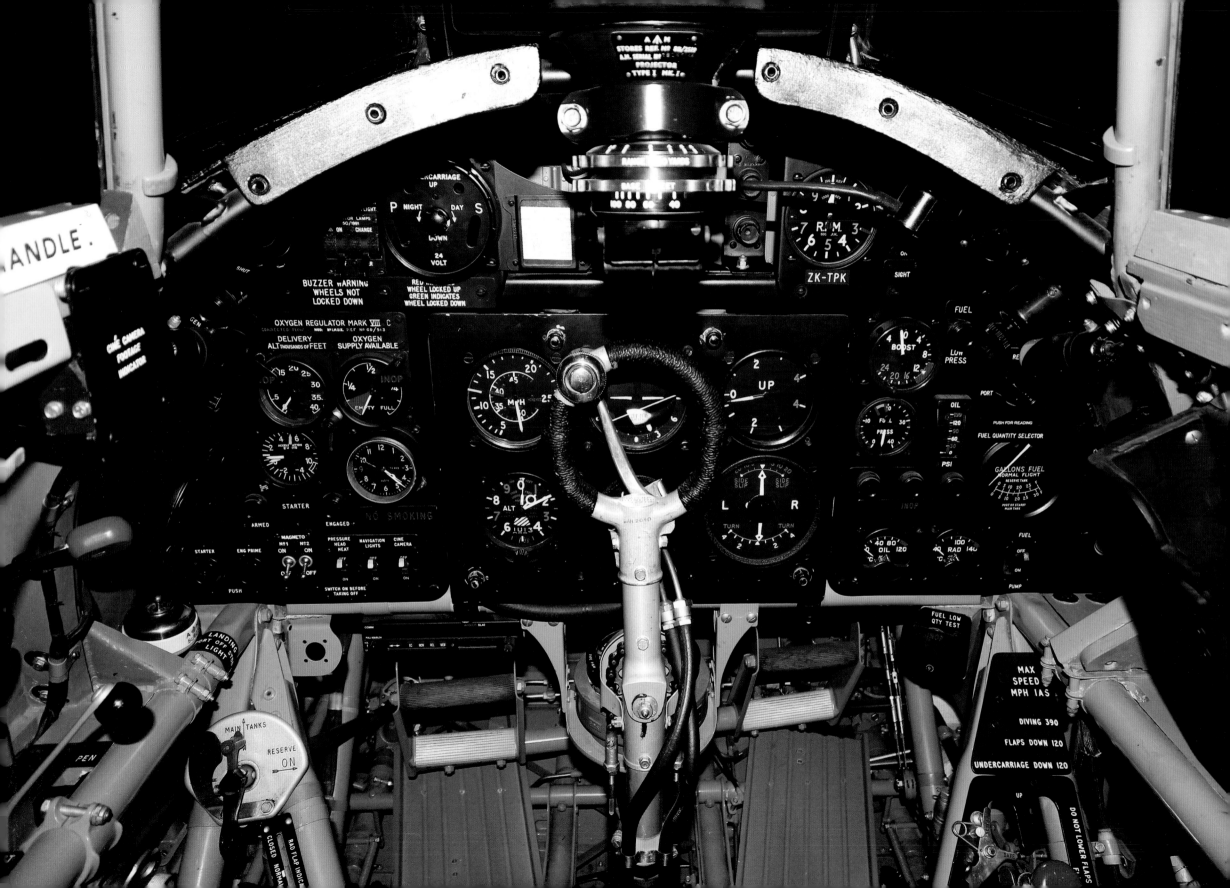

STEVE TAYLOR: HURRICANE PILOT

Being entrusted to fly a historically significant aircraft such as the Hurricane is a great privilege and that is always the most prevalent impression to me when flying these classics. The aeroplane is a tight fit for someone my size (189 cm tall) and the cockpit layout leaves a lot to be desired – it's noisy, vibrates a lot and the controls are heavy; but it's a Hurricane. Gentle aerobatics and low passes are all that are needed to display the aircraft, with the distinctive profile and beautiful sound of its V12 Merlin doing the rest. The Hurricane is fairly docile compared with other World War II fighters and is not that difficult to fly; in fact I think there is an aura of difficulty cultivated around these aeroplanes that is designed to reserve them for a few lucky pilots. I always find that pulling off a good three-point landing after a flight in a warbird is hard to beat and the Hurricane does it beautifully, not unlike the Piper Cub.

HAWKER HURRICANE Mk IIa	
LENGTH	31 ft 5 in (9.57 m)
HEIGHT	13 ft 1.5 in (4.00 m)
WINGSPAN	40 ft 4 in (12.19 m)
ENGINE	Rolls-Royce Merlin 35 V12, 1200 hp
MAXIMUM SPEED	340 mph (547 km/h)
RANGE	470 miles (756 km)
SERVICE CEILING	36,000 ft (10,980 m)
ARMAMENT	Eight 0.303 calibre machine guns

P3351 has only flown 52 hours since its restoration in the 1990's. The aircraft looks better now than when it rolled out of the factory during WWII.

Steve Taylor taxis past the crowd at Warbirds Over Wanaka 2008. This Hurricane is the only airworthy example in the Southern Hemisphere, of around twelve still flying worldwide.

SUPERMARINE
SPITFIRE Mk Vb
NX628BL (BL628 Marion)

An icon of freedom in the UK and Commonwealth, the elegant Spitfire is arguably the most widely recognised military aircraft in history; its graceful elliptical wings and slender fuselage making this fighter every inch a 'lady'.

Designed in the 1930s by Reginald Joseph Mitchell of Supermarine Aviation Works, the Spitfire was produced in greater numbers than any other British aircraft, and was the only Allied fighter in production throughout the war.

It was built in many variations, with different wing configurations, and was used well into the 1950s. During World War II it was considered by many to be the backbone of the Royal Air Force and served in several roles – fighter-bomber, reconnaissance, interceptor and trainer.

After the Battle of Britain, Supermarine began to manufacture an improved version of the Spitfire which had played such an important role in foiling Hitler's invasion plans. With the RAF tentatively going on the offensive with sorties across the Channel at the beginning of 1941, a faster and more heavily armed Spitfire was needed. This saw the introduction of the Mk Vb (the b refers to the wing armament) in February 1941, powered by the Merlin 45 and producing 1515 hp at 11,000 ft. Its main opponent over the summer of 1941 was the Messerschmitt Bf 109F which was similar in performance, although the Spitfire was more heavily armed.

The Mk V was also the first Spitfire to be modified to carry bombs and drop tanks, and the design saw the first appearance of the fighter (F) and low level fighter (LF) designations. The LF used modified engines that produced their best output at lower altitudes, and the Mk V could reach 355 mph (571 km/h) at 5900 ft (1798 m) making it faster than the Bf 109G and on a par with Fw 190. However it was the Focke Wulf Fw 190 – the so-called 'Butcher Bird' – that became the nemesis of the Mk V, and large numbers were lost to this new Luftwaffe fighter forcing a rethink of operations by Fighter Command. It wasn't until the introduction of the Mk IX in June 1942 that the advantage swung back in favour of the RAF and large fighter operations over the Continent would resume.

The Mk V was produced in greater numbers than any other single mark of Spitfire and was the first to be used in large numbers outside the UK, serving in Malta, North Africa and the Far East.

Our featured aircraft, Spitfire Mk Vb BL628, served with No. 401 (Canadian Squadron) and became the mount of G. B. 'Scotty' Murray who named the fighter 'Marion' after his girlfriend. It has come a long way since its remains were found on a farmyard in St Merryn in Cornwall, England in 1977 by two Australians, Peter Croser and Mike Aitchison. Following the construction of the fuselage by Dick Melton in the UK, the Spitfire was returned to Australia and some time later the wings were placed in the capable hands of Warren Denholm's Auckland-based Avspecs Ltd, followed at a later stage by the rest of the airframe. 'Marion' took to the skies again on 29 September 2007 and, following testing by John Lamont and Keith Skilling, the aircraft was shipped to new owner Rod Lewis of Texas.

John Lamont lands 'Marion' following another successful test flight at Ardmore airfield in September 2007. The Mk V is considered to be one of the nicest Spitfire marks to fly.

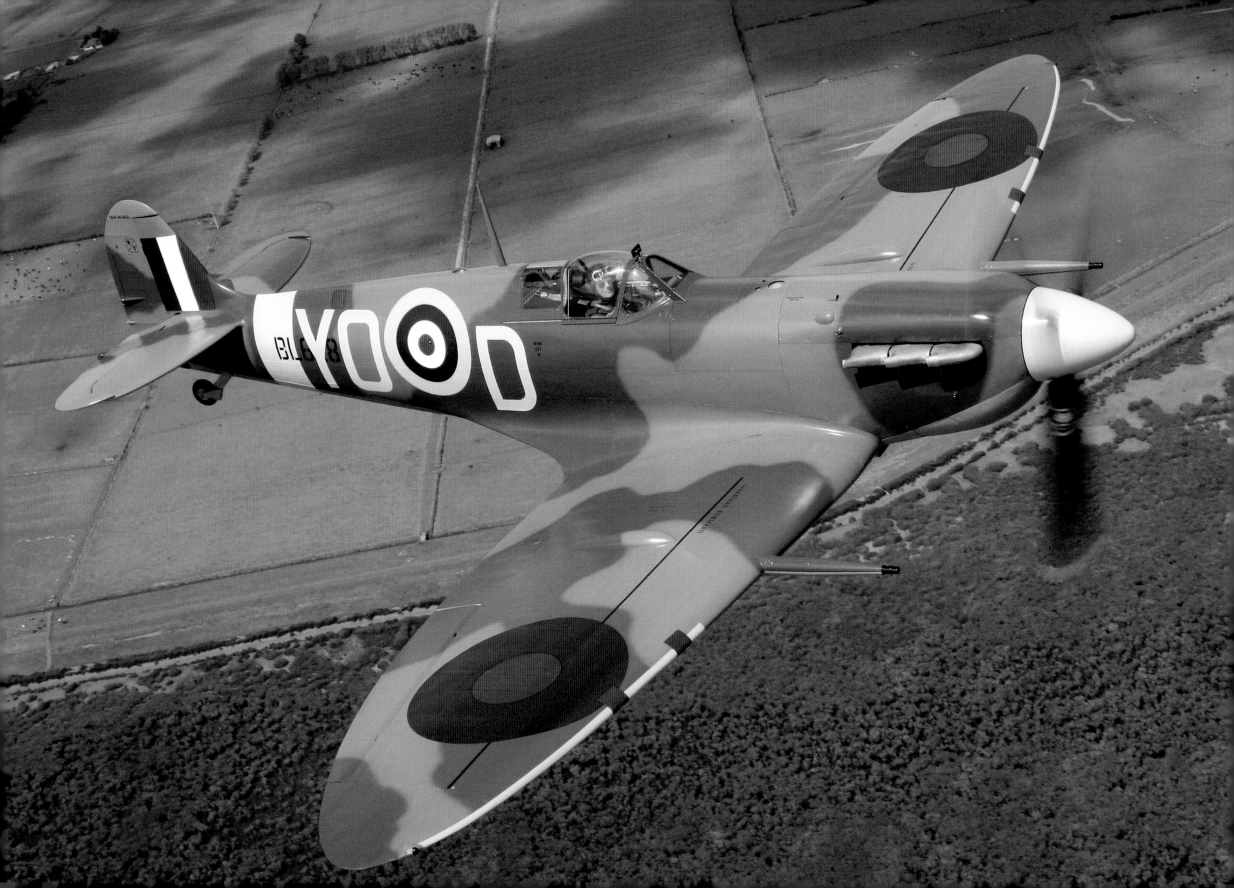

JOHN LAMONT: SPITFIRE PILOT

The Mk V Spitfire was regarded by many World War II pilots as the nicest of the type to fly, even though it was to be superseded by heavier and more powerful models. This legendary aircraft was the most prolifically produced of all the Spitfires and yet very few remain flyable today. I therefore felt very excited and privileged when asked to test fly 'Marion' in October 2007.

A 'Tiger Moth on steroids' is possibly an apt description of the Mk V. It feels light and responsive in the controls and the Merlin is very lively. The big elliptical wing and relatively light all-up weight produces exceptional turning capability and low stalling and landing speeds. At the same time the slim profile and clean lines allow very high speeds in a dive. It is a delight to aerobat and display, although like all Spits it doesn't roll very fast. Compared with other fighters of the era, the Spitfire is a simple aircraft to fly and very well mannered in all phases of flight. From the moment the Merlin belched smokily into life at start up, to the final shut down, 'Marion' lived up to all my expectations. My test flight report and log book entries from October 2007 show total flight time of 5.6 hours in the Mk V – 5.6 hours of serious work and serious delight!

SUPERMARINE SPITFIRE Mk Vb

LENGTH	29 ft 11 in (9.12 m)
HEIGHT	9 ft 11 in (3.02 m)
WINGSPAN	36 ft 10 in (11.23 m)
ENGINE	Rolls-Royce Merlin 45 V12, 1515 hp
MAXIMUM SPEED	378 mph (605 km/h)
RANGE	395 miles (635 km)
SERVICE CEILING	36,500 ft (11,125 m)
ARMAMENT	Two 20 mm cannons and four 0.303 calibre Browning machine guns

The Spitfire is widely regarded as one of the most beautiful aircraft to ever take flight. Its elliptical wings and wonderful sound also make it one of the most recognisable aeroplanes to have ever flown.

The instrument panel is quite basic in the Mk Vb Spitfire. The silver switch on the control column is the trigger for guns and cannons. The guns were synchronised to a gun camera which allowed footage to be captured each time the trigger was pushed, which helped to confirm pilot claims of enemy victories.

The Rolls-Royce Merlin engine powered Spitfires from the start and throughout World War II. This V12 engine provided a lot of power to the light airframe of the Mk Vb. This engine was totally rebuilt in the United States before being fitted in New Zealand and should see 'Marion' fly for many years to come.

SUPERMARINE
SPITFIRE Mk IX
ZK-SPI (PV270)

With the appearance of the Focke Wulf Fw 190A over the Channel Front in September 1941 it soon became apparent to the Royal Air Force that the Spitfire V was outclassed and work began with some urgency on countering the 'Butcher Bird' threat. Without the time to make major changes to the basic airframe, a 'stop-gap' measure of fitting a Merlin 61 engine to a Mk V allowed rapid development and production, until 'something better' could be produced. But, much to the delight of the Air Ministry, this was not required as the capabilities of this Spitfire were discovered to be more than adequate during test flights on 26 February 1942. Its top speed and service ceiling were faster and higher than the Mk V, and so full production got underway in June 1942 with the fighter entering service the following month.

The Mk IX's first combat success came on 30 July 1942, when one shot down a Fw 190. Among other notable achievements in its long career, the Mk IX took part in the highest altitude combat of World War II when it intercepted a German bomber – a Junkers Ju 86R – at 43,000 ft (13,106 m) over Southampton on 12 September 1942. On 5 October 1944 Spitfire Mk IXs of the Royal Canadian Air Force's 401 Squadron were the first allied aircraft to shoot down a Messerschmitt Me 262 Jet. The 'interim' Spitfire continued in service throughout the war and into the post-war era with various air forces, despite more powerful marks being available.

Not surprisingly the Mk IX was described by many of its pilots as the best of the breed and many of the RAF's fighter leaders spent a good deal of their operational careers flying the type. One of these was New Zealander Air Commodore Alan Christopher 'Al' Deere DSO, OBE, DFC & Bar, who was appointed Wing Leader at Biggin Hill near London in early 1943 and ended the war with twenty-two confirmed victories, ten probable and eighteen damaged.

Our featured aircraft, PV270, represents one of Al's fighters and was restored by Al's nephew, Brendon Deere. PV270 is a truly international fighter, having served with the RAF in North Africa and Italy, before being operated post-war by the Israeli and Burmese Air Forces. Following a final flight on 12 January 1956 the aircraft went into storage and eventually spent many years displayed on a pole as a gate guardian. In 1995 the aircraft, along with others, was moved to Mingaladon Air Force base as part of the establishment of the Burma Air Force Museum. PV270 was one of three Spitfires and one Seafire declared surplus to requirements and eventually found its way to New Zealand and a hangar at Feilding in December 2003, ready for the project start which would see the airframe returned to 'new' zero time condition. On 6 March 2009, PV270 taxied under its own power for the first time in fifty-three years – the seventieth anniversary of Al Deere's first flight in a Spitfire in March 1939. Twelve days later at RNZAF Base Ohakea, experienced warbird pilot Keith Skilling lifted PV270 off the grass for its first flight. This magnificent aircraft would make its public debut to an adoring crowd at the Classic Fighters Airshow at Omaka, Blenheim, over Easter 2009 and Brendon would later be presented with the Grand Champion Trophy – not that that was a surprise!

JOHN LANHAM: SPITFIRE PILOT

Spitfire! The word has been in my consciousness for sixty years. The first model I ever made, at about eight years old, was a Spitfire. By age ten or eleven, I could draw them in three dimensions. In my teens I knew all the names, had read all the books. The first Spitfire I ever saw flying was at an air show in England in about 1963; it was a mock dogfight between a Spitfire and a Hurricane, owned by British Aircraft Corporation and Hawker Aircraft respectively. The Hurricane was flown by Bill Bedford, the Spitfire by Geoffrey Quill, both immaculate in sports jacket and tie. Later, the two aircraft were presented to the RAF to become the beginnings of the Battle of Britain Memorial Flight. Then and since I have had the privilege of meeting some of the 'greats' associated with the aircraft – Deere, Gray, Bader, Quill, Henshaw, Stanford-Tuck and Kingcome .

Along the way I have had the good fortune to fly some fine aircraft: the Canberra, a natural successor to the de Havilland Mosquito; the A–4 Skyhawk, manoeuvrable and versatile, the fighter pilot's answer to getting a quart out of a pint pot; the North American Harvard, best fun for thirty minutes of aerobatics; the Polikarpov I–153 Chaika, the aircraft in which I have learned most about hands and feet flying; camouflaged monoplanes, silver biplanes, and multicoloured triplancs. But always, in the back of my mind, was the aspiration to fly a Spitfire.

The Spitfire is everything that is said about it – beautiful to look at, stirring to listen to, perfection to fly. Some aircraft you sit in, some you sit on. The Spitfire wraps around you; you are part of it, a fighter to go to war in. The long nose, the sound of the Merlin, the feel, the curving elliptical wings, 'the long delirious burning blue'[1] and the dream come true!

[1] From the poem 'High Flight' by John Gillespie Magee Jr, an American WWII Spitfire pilot, who wrote the poem after being inspired during a test flight of a Spitfire Mk V. Three months later, aged just nineteen, John Magee died during a non-combat air accident. After his death his poem was widely published.

Sean Perrett flies the Spitfire over its home base at RNZAF Base Ohakea. Owner Brendon Deere flies alongside in his Harvard, with Jim Rankin onboard who taught Brendon to fly this aircraft.

BRENDON DEERE: OWNER OF SPITFIRE PV270

Restoring a Spitfire is no easy task, but the work on PV270 represents an achievement I will always be proud of. The greatest pleasure I get from our Spitfire is the feedback from people wherever we show who come up and tell us about the memories it brings back, or the emotions it evokes. I think my Uncle Al would have been very pleased to see a Spitfire in his Biggin Hill markings again, and with the end result after over five years of restoration. I never tire of watching and listening to it fly, and I am reminded each time that for many people it is the first time they have seen and heard a Spitfire; that always brings a smile to my face. We went to a lot of trouble to keep the aircraft authentic and at times during the restoration it felt like we had created too much work for ourselves. But it is a special pleasure to know that the aircraft is as close to the original as when it first left the Castle Bromwich factory back in September 1944. In that way I see it as a real time machine that stretches back to Biggin Hill or any other RAF Spitfire station.

SEAN PERRETT: SPITFIRE PILOT

The Mk IX Spitfire was arguably the finest fighter of its day. Its beautiful shape belied the fact that it was an airborne assassin. It is a huge honour to fly the Spitfire and each time I strap into the cockpit, I think of the young Allied Spitfire pilots during the war. Many of them were inexperienced teenagers who must have been very apprehensive every time they went into combat.

Flying the Spitfire is a delight. Despite its high performance, it has very docile handling characteristics and you instantly feel at one with the aircraft. In the cockpit, you are treated to the roar of the Rolls-Royce Merlin engine and the unrivalled view of the elliptical wings.

The Spitfire has to be the easiest aircraft I have had the pleasure to display. With its stunning shape and the distinctive sound of the Merlin, all you have to do is show up at an air show and watch and hear it fly!

SUPERMARINE SPITFIRE Mk IX	
LENGTH	31 ft 3 in (9.52 m)
HEIGHT	11 ft 9 in (3.58 m)
WINGSPAN	36 ft 10 in (11.23 m)
ENGINE	Rolls-Royce Merlin 61 V12, 1565 hp
MAXIMUM SPEED	408 mph (657 km/h)
RANGE	434 miles (698 km)
SERVICE CEILING	43,000 ft (13,106 m)
ARMAMENT	Two 20 mm cannons and four 0.303 calibre Browning machine guns

As you can see from this view, visibility from a Spitfire on the ground can make handling difficult. If you see a Spitfire weaving from side to side during taxiing, the pilot is doing this so he can peer around the windscreen to avoid obstacles.

Four F-18 Hornets streak past the Spitfire at Warbirds Over Wanaka 2010 demonstrating how far technology has come since WWII. The Hornet cruises faster than the Spitfire's maximum speed.

SUPERMARINE
SPITFIRE Tr IX
ZK-WDQ (MH367)

The idea of developing a twin-seat trainer version of the legendary Spitfire was first introduced in 1941, but was deemed unnecessary, and it was in the main a product of the immediate post-war. That said, a handful were modified during the war to accommodate two pilots. One of these was by the Soviet Air Force, whose aircraft had the original front cockpit with the rear fuselage cut down to allow for the second cockpit, with glass linking the two.

After the end of the war, the idea was revived by Vickers, and in 1946 a Mk VIII was converted as a demonstrator. Remarkably the aircraft survives today. The Vickers conversion was more complex than the Russians', and saw the front cockpit moved thirteen inches forward with a large bubble canopy behind which allowed the instructor to raise his seat high in order to keep a close eye on the student pilot in the front. Although very practical it did take away some of the classic lines of the Spitfire. It was followed in 1948 by ten Spitfire T Mk IXs which were exported to India.

In 1951 a further six were converted to train pilots for the Irish Air Corps Seafire (Navy version of the Spitfire) fleet. The aircraft were used to provide transition training including gunnery practice; thereafter most were passed to the ground technical training school at Baldonnel in Ireland, where they were used as instructional airframes for the training of aircraft engineers for the Air Corps.

Our featured aircraft MH367 was built in the UK workshops of Dick Melton. Prior to a sale to Peter Godfrey in the US, who required that the airframe have some thread of Royal Air Force provenance, the front fuselage of Spitfire MH367 was acquired and retrospectively incorporated into the aircraft. Finding components to convert a single seat Spitfire to a two seat machine is a very difficult task but for MH367 it was a bit easier due to many parts secured from a two seat aircraft imported into the USA that was converted back to a single seat aircraft. The remainder of the rebuild was undertaken by Harry Stenger in Florida and the Spitfire first flew in September 2007. Soon after the aircraft was sold to Doug Brooker of Auckland and it is now displayed in the Desert Air Force colours of New Zealand's highest scoring ace, Wing Commander Colin Gray, who finished the war with 27.5 kills.

The conversion is aesthetically pleasing and very practical as the aircraft can be flown from the front or rear seat. Doug Brooker is an accomplished aerobatic pilot who flies the Spitfire at air shows all over New Zealand.

DOUG BROOKER: SPITFIRE OWNER AND PILOT

My enthusiasm for the Spitfire originated while reading Biggles books as a boy. However, until I imported this Spitfire into New Zealand, I had no idea of the immense general public interest in them. I have since received many messages, calls and emails from complete strangers, and the level of interest is absolutely amazing.

To truly appreciate the aeroplane requires an appreciation of its history – to hear the noise, to look at the wings, to strap into the compact cockpit, to look through the armour plated glass windshield, and to smell the smell.

How is it to fly? It is certainly not the same as the modern high performance aerobatic aircraft that I am so familiar with. At over three tons it is much heavier on the ailerons, but it does have a very powerful elevator making it easy to pull high g loads. This, along with the superb elliptical wing, gives it an incredibly tight turning circle. To quote Squadron Leader Colin Gray, 'There was no way a Fw 190 could turn inside a Spitfire'. At low cruise power it is very comfortable and stable. High power is a whole different thing. The throbbing engine, the surge in speed and the change in trim, leaves you with no doubt that it means business. The whole Spitfire experience – it's great!

KEITH SKILLING: SPITFIRE PILOT

If it looks right it will fly right, and this is so true of the Spitfire. I could write for hours on the joys of flying a Spitfire, but it has all been said before. Its designer Mitchell got it just right, producing a very docile and forgiving aircraft, but with the Rolls-Royce Merlin wound up to 2850 rpm plus 12 inches of manifold pressure (max climb), it really comes alive and turns into a very mean fighting machine. The cockpit is surprisingly simple, with the combination of a great engine and lovely controls. It is a little light on the elevators so all of this makes the Spitfire one of the best fighters of all time. No wonder the young pilots in WWII felt invincible in this aircraft.

Two-seat Spitfires are very rare and we are fortunate to have one flying in New Zealand thanks to Doug Brooker's vision. It also allows for very lucky passengers to go for the flight of a lifetime.

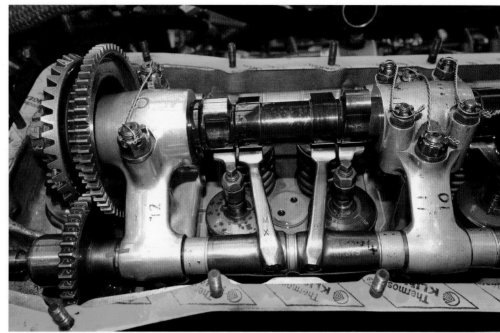

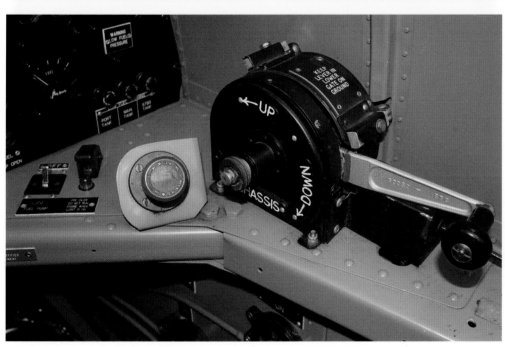

SUPERMARINE SPITFIRE Tr IX

LENGTH	31 ft 3 in (9.52 m)
HEIGHT	11 ft 9 in (3.58 m)
WINGSPAN	36 ft 10 in (11.23 m)
ENGINE	Rolls Packard Merlin 266 V12, 1710 hp
MAXIMUM SPEED	408 mph (657 km/h)
RANGE	434 miles (698 km)
SERVICE CEILING	43,000 ft (13,106 m)
ARMAMENT	Two 20 mm cannons and four 0.303 calibre Browning machine guns

This aircraft has dual controls so both occupants can share in flying the Spitfire. Both cockpits have the single-seat Spitfire layout and allow for future pilots to be trained in flying this iconic aircraft.

ABOVE The Spitfire breaks and heads for home following a photoshoot. Doug Brooker actively flies
this aircraft and can be seen thrilling crowds at airshows all over New Zealand.
OPPOSITE The Spitfire Tr IX with a P–51D Mustang.

FOCKE WULF
Fw 190 A8/N
ZK-RFR 990001

In September 1941 four radial-engined aircraft from JG26 – a Luftwaffe fighter wing – bounced a group of Spitfires and scored three kills. The aircraft they flew were fast, powerful and agile, with an impressive rate of roll and superb take-off and landing characteristics.

The Focke Wulf Fw 190 – which would become known as the 'Butcher Bird' to the Allies – had arrived and the new fighter quickly began to rule the skies in the West, proving itself superior in almost all aspects to the RAF's main front-line fighter, the Spitfire Mk V. Used by the Germans as a workhorse in the war, it was suitable as a day fighter, ground-attack aircraft and to a lesser degree as a night fighter.

The British decided they needed to steal an example for study, and a Commando operation was planned, codenamed Operation Air Thief. Fortunately this proved unnecessary when an example landed on an RAF airfield by mistake in June 1942. It wasn't until the introduction of the Spitfire Mk IX that the Butcher Bird's air superiority was reined in and the cut and thrust of aerial combat came down to piloting skills and no small amount of luck.

By war's end some 20,000 Fw 190s of all models had been produced; however few survived and up until very recently there was little chance of seeing one back in the skies.

This was to change, however, through the determination and sheer hard work of Claus Colling, the late Hans Wildmoser and a small but dedicated team who collectively worked under the banner of Flug Werk, based in Bavaria in Germany. Their aim, to recreate the Fw 190, began in June 1996 after many years of data gathering.

But the long road to a finished aircraft was not an easy one by any means and saw the firm mastering a seemingly endless list of tasks, hurdles and set-backs. Components were manufactured in seven countries, and Aerostar in Romania set up a limited production run manufacturing fuselage and wing structures on behalf of Flug Werk. These were built using original drawings and reverse engineering which saw about 3.5 tons of original Fw 190 wreckage used to gather critical measurements.

In the interest of flight safety, or perhaps the lack of original or similar system components, some of the systems were redesigned. This applied mainly to the fuel and oil system, the cooling of the latter being a major headache, and similar to the problem faced by the original designers.

A major task was to fit a suitable engine to the airframe and without the original BMW 801, the Russian-designed ASh–82T was found to be a worthy substitute. It has the same weight, diameter, length and swept volume as the BMW and is also direct fuel-injected. All the effort culminated on 22 June 2004 when a Fw 190 took to the skies over Germany for the first time since 1945.

The aircraft were sold exclusively as kits and it is not only the warbird fraternity that has benefitted from the Flug Werk initiative, with airframes filling important gaps in several museums. By the time Flug Werk decided to terminate the project and advertised the sale of their vast inventory of related tools, jigs, drawings and manufacturing rights in January 2011, twenty-one aircraft had been completed, mostly the short nose Fw 190 A8/N (N= Nachbau or replica) but with a handful of long nose Fw 190 D9/Ns as well.

The Fw 190 basks in the sun just days before its first flight in New Zealand. This view shows that the aircraft sits quite high despite the forward stagger of the main undercarriage. The canopy has been 'blown' so the tall owner can eventually fly the aircraft.

The ASh–82T engine at full power during test runs before first flight. The ground vibrated as the 1850 hp engine was held wide open to ensure maximum performance was achieved before first flight.

FRANK PARKER: Fw 190 PILOT

I felt privileged to be asked to fly the 'Chariots of Fire' Flug Werk Fw 190. Before taking on a task of this significance it was appropriate to research the aircraft and its heritage. The Flug Werk story covers some fifteen years and the extent of their achievement in bringing a reproduction of the Fw 190 to reality has been well documented.

The first impression of the aircraft with its somewhat ungainly 'stance' is one of aggression. This was borne out in its early successes in the skies over Europe in 1941; in fact it reigned supreme for over twelve months in a rapidly developing aviation environment. With developments as fighter, bomber and ground-attack variants it is generally regarded as Germany's most successful World War II aircraft.

This Flug Werk aircraft is a faithful reproduction from original plans and incorporates a few genuine 1940 vintage components.

Any 1940s vintage front-line fighter is a serious aircraft and the Fw 190 fits this category. The ASh–82T engine enthuses 'attitude'; the aircraft with no armament has a spirited performance. While we have only had the opportunity for initial evaluation the aircraft has its own persona. It is not the classical harmony of the P–40, the light elevators of the Spitfire, nor the nimbleness of the Yak 3. The engine brings the feel of the Lavochkin La–9; however, the flight controls are unique to this aircraft, light, neutral with little feedback to the pilot. It's not love at first flight, but with a little more exposure this will become a 'nice' aircraft to fly. I can't wait!

FOCKE WULF Fw 190 A8/N	
LENGTH	29 ft 5 in (9.0 m)
HEIGHT	13 ft (3.92 m)
WINGSPAN	34 ft 5 in (10.51 m)
ENGINE	Shetsov ASh–82T, 14 cylinder radial, 1850 hp
MAXIMUM SPEED	408 mph (656 km)
RANGE	500 miles (804 km)
SERVICE CEILING	37,430 ft (11,410 m)
ARMAMENT	Two 7.92 mm guns in the nose, up to four 20 mm guns in the wings

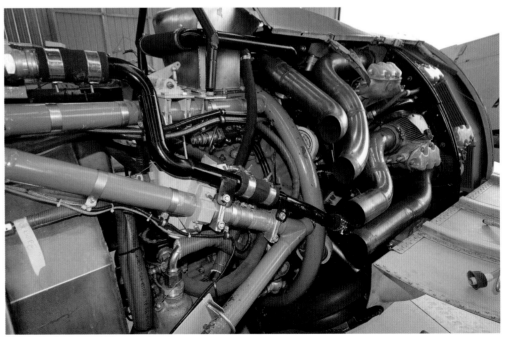

JAY MCINTYRE: MANAGING DIRECTOR OF JEM AVIATION

This magnificent aeroplane, S/No 990001 / ex D-FWWC was the first of the Flug Werk reproductions to be completed back in 2004. Initial test flying and proving of the design saw test flying partially completed in 2007 before '01 was set aside while Flug Werk concentrated on getting the remaining airframe/engine kits out to their customers.

In 2009 the aircraft was sold to a New Zealand owner and Flug Werk commenced returning the aircraft to an airworthy state, '01 having been somewhat cannibalised in order to meet customer deadlines. This time was also used to upgrade some of the systems that had been found deficient during test flying such as the wheel brakes and oil cooler efficiency.

By mid 2010 '01 was ready to fly again but an unfortunate incident with a sister ship saw the Flug Werk fleet grounded while propeller defects were investigated. By the time this was sorted out a particularly vicious European winter had set in and with no hope of any meaningful test flying being completed the decision to ship the aircraft to its new home at Omaka was undertaken. At the end of January 2011 the aircraft, christened 'Storm of Steel' by her owner, was finally bound for New Zealand. A period of trying patience followed as all involved hoped the aircraft would arrive with enough time to allow for assembly, certification and test flying in the hope that she could be displayed at the forthcoming Easter 2011 Classic Fighters Airshow. After some frustrating delays the aircraft was delivered to JEM Aviation's premises on a cold rainy morning, approximately two weeks behind schedule. Things were going to be tight, but in what seems to be the tradition of Kiwi airshows, we were not about to let that stop us!

Two hours after arrival the entire aircraft had been disgorged from the container and work was underway on a thorough inspection of all components prior to assembly. Unfortunately the aircraft had suffered some transit damage during its eight weeks at sea. Luckily it all proved relatively minor, although it did slow things down another few days. A few days later with the help of Dean's Lifting Services we successfully mated the fuselage to the wing in a process that was completed in time for lunch. One could really see the menacing lines of the Fw 190 starting to appear! Five days and 60 litres of oil later, we carried out the initial engine runs. That was an awesome moment as the aircraft is a typical noisy, smoky World War II aeroplane. With 1850 hp up front, the feeling of power was just amazing!

Finally, the big day came and on the 20th of April Frank took ZK-RFR for what is probably the first flight of a Fw 190 in the Southern Hemisphere. After some 20 minutes overhead the airfield, some circuits were undertaken at nearby Woodbourne with its longer runways. All having gone well, Frank returned to Omaka where to everyone's dismay, the right hand gear leg failed to extend. After circling overhead the leg was eventually extended and a successful landing made. With the exception of that, Frank was very happy with the aircraft, the only other problems being aileron and rudder trims needing adjustment and a 'noisy' radio.

More test flights were undertaken with Frank continuing to expand the envelope. Spectators were even treated to some gentle aerobatics high above Omaka on the day before Good Friday.

Good Friday turned out to be not so good. Frank had departed on another flight and about 40 minutes into it noted a new vibration from 'up front'. Whilst returning to the airfield he heard two loud reports and requested a priority landing. Upon shut down we noted that the aircraft was 'mortally wounded' with large chunks missing from two of the propeller blades. These were quickly traced to two missing cooling fan blades behind the prop that had, for some reason, rubbed on the inside of the cowling nose ring and sheared off, the propeller blades being their final destination.

With that, the aircraft was relegated to static display only at Classic Fighters 2011. However, the few flights that were made certainly have everyone keen to see more!

Since Easter the propeller blades have been returned to the manufacturer for repair. While this is underway, the time will be taken to manufacture and fit the lower gear doors, fit the tailwheel retraction mechanism, fit and plumb the centreline fuel tank and tend to a myriad of small tidying up jobs.

We are hoping to have 'Storm of Steel' back in the air by September.

The Fw 190 still carries German language signage inside the cockpit so a lot of study was needed by Jay and Frank before first flight. The cockpit is well fitted out and quite a snug fit.

GOODYEAR
FG-1D CORSAIR
ZK-COR (NZ5648)

With its distinctive 'inverted gull wings' the powerful Navy and Marine Corsair is the most easily recognisable aircraft of the war era. Originally developed for the US Navy in 1938 by manufacturers Vought, the F4U incorporated the largest engine available at the time, the 2000 hp Pratt & Whitney R-2800 Double Wasp radial. When demand for the aircraft overwhelmed Vought's capability, Goodyear and Brewster began producing them. Those built by Goodyear were designated FG; Brewster models were F3A 1.

To accommodate a folding wing, the designers had considered retracting the main landing gear rearward, but for the chord of wing selected, it was difficult to fit undercarriage struts long enough to provide enough clearance for the large propeller. The solution was an inverted gull wing, which, while it solved the problem, also meant it was heavier and more complicated to manufacture than the conventional wing.

The prototype first flew in May 1940, becoming the first single-engine US fighter to fly faster than 400 mph (640 km/h) in straight and level flight. Because of its advances in technology and a top speed greater than existing Navy aircraft, numerous technical problems had to be solved before the Corsair could enter service. The aircraft was not considered fit for carrier use until wing stall problems and the deck 'bounce' on landing could be solved; this did not happen until 1944.

In the meantime the US Marines welcomed the new fighter and from February 1943, Corsairs were in action from island-based strips in the Solomons, often in the ground attack role which they were hugely effective in. Tactics to best combat the nimble Japanese Zeros were soon worked out – the main lesson being not to engage the Zero at slow speeds and maintain an altitude advantage whenever possible.

By late 1943 the US Navy finally got into combat using the Corsair, albeit with only two units. However once it was cleared for large deployment in April 1944 – following the fitting of a longer oleo strut, or shock absorber, to eliminate the bounce problem – operations from both land and sea stepped up in intensity. It was around this time that Goodyear and Brewster began production. By the end of the war the Corsair had claimed over 2140 victories against Japanese aircraft, whilst losing 'only' 189.

Over 12,500 examples of the Corsair were built between 1942 and 1952. They went on to serve during the Korean War and more localised conflicts in the Middle East and South America – notably the so-called 'Soccer War' between Honduras and El Salvador in 1969 which saw Corsair combat Corsair, as both countries operated the type.

The Royal New Zealand Air Force was supplied with 424 Corsairs in 1944 to replace their P–40 Kittyhawks and the featured aircraft, NZ5648, is the sole airworthy survivor of these. It served with the RNZAF from August 1945 to May 1948 before being sold as scrap. Rescued from a Rukuhia scrapyard and restored to taxiing condition in the 1960s, it was soon sold to a buyer in the US. Arriving in the UK for Warbirds of Great Britain in 1988, the aircraft then went to the famous Old Flying Machine Company at Duxford in Cambridgeshire, England. This is the company founded by New Zealand-born fighter pilot Ray Hanna – one of the founding members of the Red Arrows. There it was presented once again wearing RNZAF colours for a period, and by the time it returned to New Zealand in 2004 it was back in a United States Marine Corps scheme, that of VF–17 'Jolly Rogers'. Now owned by the Old Stick & Rudder Co., it is based at Hood Aerodrome, Masterton, and is a regular airshow performer. Roughly thirty airworthy Corsairs have survived worldwide with the majority of them flying in the US. We are extremely lucky to have this one flying in New Zealand.

Keith Skilling lines up behind a RNZAF C-130 Hercules during Warbirds Over Wanaka 2008. A 2000 hp engine needs a large diameter propeller which must have clearance whilst on the ground. This was achieved by development of the distinctive gull wing design.

ABOVE The Corsair was the first WWII fighter to achieve 400 mph in level flight. Keith Skilling dives for the display line with contrails visible on both wingtips.
OPPOSITE The Corsair with a P–40E Kittyhawk.

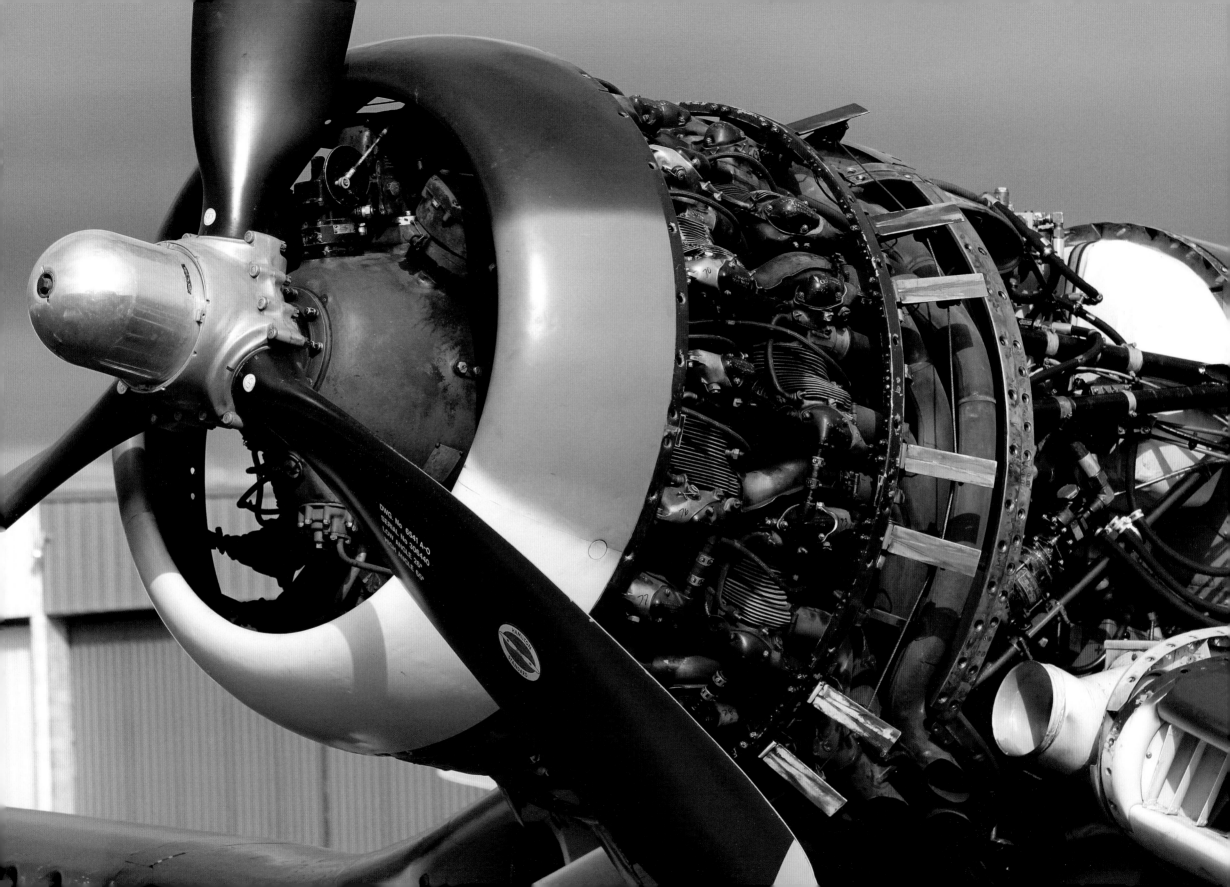

OPPOSITE The Corsair's huge 18 cylinder Pratt & Whitney Double Wasp radial engine.

KEITH SKILLING: CORSAIR PILOT

I first flew this particular Corsair in 1994 on a flight across Europe accompanying Mark Hanna (son of Ray) in his Spitfire to an air show in Warsaw. We returned a week later via an air show at Halle-Oppin in Germany, and for the whole journey I was regaled with a running history lesson of both WW1 and WWII from Mark. I will never forget it. So started a wonderful relationship with this magnificent aeroplane. For the next nine years I flew it in Europe, culminating in five years with the Breitling Fighters Display Team in Duxford. Thankfully Ray Hanna returned it home to New Zealand in 2004. While the Corsair was late to arrive into World War II, it is now generally recognised as the best fighter of the era below 15,000 feet. Despite its appearance, it is hugely powerful, manoeuvrable and reliable. The huge Pratt & Whitney is a little hard to start but once it gets going it is very smooth and has never let me down. Yet. It won't out-turn a Spitfire, but with 2000 hp, it can certainly outrun it! The Corsair has beautifully harmonised controls that remain very light throughout the whole speed range. Vought spent hundreds of hours during test flying to get them just right. The pilot's seating position is not the most comfortable but I like to sit high and that gives me a good view and a great feeling of control.

All of this really adds up to the Corsair being a great aircraft to fly and display. I just love it!

GOODYEAR FG–1D CORSAIR

LENGTH	33 ft 4 in (10.1 m)
HEIGHT	14 ft 9 in (4.5 m)
WINGSPAN	41 ft (12.5 m)
ENGINE	Pratt & Whitney R-2800-8, 18 cylinder radial, 2000 hp
MAXIMUM SPEED	417 mph (671 km/h)
RANGE	1015 miles (1633 km)
SERVICE CEILING	36,900 ft (11,247 m)
ARMAMENT	Six Browning 0.50 calibre machine guns

The Corsair's wing-folding mechanism allowed many more aircraft to be fitted onto aircraft carriers during WWII.
Keith Skilling demonstrates the wing folding at Warbirds Over Wanaka 2010.

GENE DeMARCO: CORSAIR PILOT

Aside from the plastic models I pieced together as a kid, my earliest Corsair memories are of reading about Marine Fighter Ace Greg 'Pappy' Boyington and his exploits in command of the famed Black Sheep Squadron, in the book *Baa Baa Black Sheep* and in the TV series of the same name.

Years later when the opportunity came to actually fly a Corsair, I called another fellow American for some bent-winged-bird advice. 'You'll love it!' he said 'You won't have any problem!' Then he proceeded in a very 'Pappy' Boyington sort of way to add a few things I might have a problem with if I didn't pay particular attention to the wing locking mechanism before take-off. 'If only one wing is locked ... you will have a helluva roll rate. If both wings are unlocked ... then you'll have a helluva sink rate.'

The Corsair was the first single-engine production aircraft capable of 400 mph in level flight. With its characteristic gull wing and giant 18 cylinder double wasp radial, it proved a superb fighter in the Pacific campaign and achieved a victory ratio approaching 10 to 1. The last surviving Corsair to have served with the RNZAF in the Pacific during WWII is NZ5648 or 'Josephine' as she has been affectionately known for many years. One of my most vivid flying memories was my first flight in this particular aircraft not because of some near death experience or narrow escape but because it was a perfect day to fly in an aeroplane that exceeded all of my expectations!

Prior to getting the machine in the air however, I had to figure out the starting procedure. Nothing as simple as a push of a button or the twist of a key, just a mere 17 steps in the pilot's manual ... and some very BOLD type spelling out all kinds of warnings and dangers if the engine doesn't start.

Take off is relatively simple. A few degrees of flaps, tail wheel locked, slowly advancing the power to 38 inches of manifold pressure (boost) and release the brakes; hold the stick back and add right rudder to counteract the torque. As the speed increases, reduce the back pressure on the stick, let the tail rise and fly away, establish the climb attitude and the speed should stabilize at about 125 mph.

The big 2000 hp Pratt & Whitney 2800 begs to be opened up to 54 inches of manifold pressure, or full power, but we preserve the engine and treat this old girl with respect and rarely exceed 38 inches. Even this is an impressive power setting. The brakes won't hold her back at this – you have nearly 10,000 lbs skidding along the seal just prior to releasing the brakes and a good deal of right-hand rudder to counteract the torque of the huge engine and big prop.

As with any aircraft it is other pilots who remind you about the things you shouldn't do, mostly because they have tried them and the result wasn't good. In the Corsair, you quickly notice the Landing Gear handle has a number of positions. One is the 'Dive Brake' setting which allows only the main gear to be extended without the tail-wheel (designed to limit the aircraft's dive speed to around 350 knots) ... this setting shouldn't be used for landing! Thanks again Larry.

Landing is usually the exciting part of any first flight. With the Corsair and its extra long nose, visibility forward and down is less than ideal so peripheral vision is a must but even that is obscured if you open the cowl flaps. Not surprisingly, fighter pilots expressed their doubts when the Corsair was first introduced as a carrier aircraft but the curved approach was quickly adapted for deck landings.

The big heavy aircraft has some unusual stall characteristics so it's best to keep the speed a bit high on approach and let the huge flaps do the work – be careful though, going around isn't the easiest with a full 50 degrees!

I was adequately warned about adding too much power too quickly in the Corsair. If you are at low airspeed, low altitude, low power and pour on the coal, the 2000 hp engine and all its torque overpowers the aileron control and wants to roll the aircraft to the left. Not good if you don't have the altitude to recover. Torque though, and all its bad effects was something I was well used to after years of flying the Sopwith Camel and other rotary engine WWI types. On that summer evening, sitting behind such a big round engine cruising at nearly 200 mph with the canopy open and the prop turning a lazy 1350 rpm, I had time to think what a thoroughly enjoyable ride and realise how fortunate I was to fly this almost 70 year old aircraft in a time of peace.

A lot of credit has to go to the people who preserve and keep aircraft like the Corsair in the air where they belong. After all, we are just caretakers of these things. They should be shared and passed down from generation to generation to remember, commemorate and enjoy. They are works of art, a testament to technology and symbols of conflict, patriotism and hope.

It is in the air that these machines must be enjoyed, in the medium they were designed to operate, in flight.

MITSUBISHI
A6M3 ZERO
NX712Z (X-133)

Ask anyone with even a basic knowledge of aviation to name a Japanese fighter and the answer will surely be 'Zero'. One of World War II's most iconic aircraft and a symbol of Imperial Japan's air power, the Mitsubishi A6M was produced in greater numbers than any other Japanese aircraft with just under 11,000 built, including trainer and seaplane versions.

Designed to fill a specific order from the Japanese Navy, initial trials were completed successfully by mid-1940 and several pre-production A6M2s were sent for combat evaluation in China where they demonstrated a marked superiority over enemy aircraft, particularly manoeuvrability – something that would remain throughout the first years of WWII. Accepted by the Navy, production proper began in July and it was during manufacture that the rear spar was reinforced and manually folding wingtips were incorporated to allow clearance on the carriers' deck elevators. Designated Navy Type 0 Carrier Fighter Model 21 – from where the name Zero came – it was this version that was available for the attack on Pearl Harbour and the early war campaigns. Although relatively low powered, its maximum speed of 330 mph at 14,950 ft, excellent climb rate, huge range, unmatched manoeuvrability and a good armament, saw the Zero come as somewhat of a shock to the Allies – it possessed an ascendancy over any other fighter type that could be ranged against it. However some of these attributes were at the expense of pilot safety – the lightweight airframe devoid of pilot armour and self-sealing fuel tanks meant many were lost over the following years to only a few rounds of ammunition before becoming immediate 'flamers'.

The Zero was an effective fighter but, as the war progressed and more powerful, better armoured and armed Allied fighters were introduced, the frailties of the Zero became all too evident. By 1944 many were operating from land bases as the Japanese Navy had lost most of its carriers and for that matter most of its experienced pilots. Many of those that were left would find themselves sacrificing both themselves and their Zeros on kamikaze missions.

Only one genuine Zero powered by a Sakae engine is airworthy today and is owned and flown by the Planes of Fame Air Museum in Chino, California. Our featured Zero was recovered from Babo in New Guinea in 1991, partially restored from several A6M3s in Russia, and then brought to the United States for completion.

Today it's operated by the Southern California wing of the Commemorative Air Force (CAF) and was shipped to New Zealand especially for display at Warbirds Over Wanaka in 2010.

The Zero has a very complex wing, meaning it is difficult to disassemble; so the aircraft was shipped to New Zealand in one piece, unloaded at Tauranga, test flown and then headed to Wanaka. Powered by a Pratt & Whitney R1830 engine, it was flown at the show by American warbird pilots Stephen Barber and Jason Somes; both aircraft and pilots proving very popular with the crowd of thousands. A special well done must go to the organisers of Warbirds Over Wanaka for bringing such a rare aeroplane here, and to the CAF for allowing the aircraft to display in New Zealand.

This could almost be a scene straight out of WWII. Frank Parker lines up the Zero in his P–40N Kittyhawk at Warbirds Over Wanaka. Stephen Barber is doing his best to evade Frank over Lake Wanaka. These two aircraft were fierce opponents during WWII.

The A6M3 Zero is a simple airplane, designed so that a low-time pilot could handle it, and an experienced pilot could make it very combat effective during the early stages of the war before faster, heavier aircraft came along. Below 220 knots, nothing of that era can out-climb, out-turn nor roll faster. It will turn on a dime, and the roll rate is very impressive for an aircraft with such long wings.

The cockpit layout is standard for that time; controls are scattered all over the place. With the machine gun breeches located in the instrument panel, one can only imagine the noise and smoke that must have been unsettling to the new pilot the first time he fired his weapons!

Being very light (approximately 4600 lbs) the Zero accelerates very rapidly right up to 200 knots, and then it's as if an anchor is deployed. Anything above that in level flight is almost impossible to achieve. The ailerons get very heavy above 200 knots, and the elevators become heavy as well. In a protracted dog fight, I'm sure the pilot would be sweating a great deal from not only fear but from physically horsing the Zero through the sky.

It has very good slow speed handling characteristics as it was meant to operate from aircraft carriers. One unusual thing is when the flaps are deployed; there is an interconnection with the ailerons that through some mysterious monkey motion limits their effectiveness on the approach. I'm told this was added for fear that green pilots might over control the bank while approaching the carrier for landing.

After flying the Zero for over seven years, I can say it is a pleasure and a privilege to have this opportunity to be a small part of history.

MITSUBISHI A6M3 ZERO

LENGTH	29 ft 9 in (9.06 m)
HEIGHT	10 ft (3.05 m)
WINGSPAN	39 ft 4 in (12 m)
ENGINE	Pratt & Whitney R1830, 14 cylinder radial, 1200 hp
MAXIMUM SPEED	330 mph (533 km/h)
RANGE	975 miles (1569 km)
SERVICE CEILING	33,000 ft (10,065 m)
ARMAMENT	Two 7.7 mm Type 97 machine guns in the nose, two 20 mm cannons in the wings

The Zero was an extremely agile fighter but as the war progressed, aircraft like the Corsair could out-run it. However Corsair pilots would never try to out-turn a Zero which was superior in this respect. The Zero was light due to no self-sealing fuel tanks and little or no armour, so a good two second burst from a Corsair's guns was often enough to bring one down.

Jason Somes from the United States flies low and fast down the runway in the days leading up to Warbirds Over Wanaka 2010.
The organisers of the show shipped the aircraft out from the United States especially for the show.

CURTISS
P-40E KITTYHAWK
ZK-RMH (NZ3009)

Serving in virtually every theatre of World War II, the Curtiss P–40 fighter was the mainstay of the United States Army Air Force during the early years of the war and would fight under various names – the Tomahawk, Warhawk and Kittyhawk. Developed from the P–36 'Hawk' series of fighters, but built around the inline Allison V–12 engine, the prototype first flew in 1938 and in spite of a less than spectacular performance at higher altitude, went into production the following year. Despite its shortcomings compared with its main adversaries, the P–40 soon built a reputation of ruggedness (a strong five spar wing contributing to this) and dependability in the harshest conditions.

Hard-learned lessons saw tactics developed that would see it become a threat to more capable adversaries. It was however far more comfortable in the North African, Russian, and Chinese Pacific theatres, where combat under 15,000 ft (4572 m) was the order of the day. It could hold its own with pilots flying to the aircraft strengths – fast 'downhill' and good high-speed manoeuvrability. In fact it would perform better than many have since given the type credit for. In an attempt to improve higher altitude performance a Rolls-Royce Merlin was fitted and this became the P–40F. However the Allison returned for subsequent models, the last production version being the P–40N which featured a stretched rear fuselage to counter the torque of the larger, late-war Allison engine which gave the aircraft a maximum speed of 378 mph (608 km/h) at 15,000 ft (4572 m).

Arguably the most famous unit to fly the fighter was the 'Flying Tigers', the popular name given to the 1st American Volunteer Group. Officially part of Republic of China Air Force, these 'volunteers' were recruited from the ranks of US aviators and were paid good salaries. The unit was commanded by Major General Claire Chennault, an American military aviator who had moved to China in 1937 after he retired. The exploits of the Flying Tigers – and the widely recognisable shark's mouth painted onto the plane – featured heavily in US propaganda newsreels, making their aircraft widely recognisable and much imitated.

Initially built for the British Royal Air Force, this P–40 was 'commandeered' by the United States Army Air Force following the attack on Pearl Harbour in 1941 and was assigned to the 68th Fighter Squadron. However it was soon after transferred to the Royal New Zealand Air Force – one of the first batch of the eventual 297 to serve from 1942–46. Allocated NZ3009 it served on the 'home front' with Nos 14 and 17 Squadrons and finally No. 2 Operational Training Unit. Post-war it languished in the Rukuhia scrapyard along with many others of the type. Fortunately it was rescued by author and aircraft restorer Charles Darby in 1959 when he and a group of young lads managed to come up with enough cash to secure the P–40, taking the most easily accessible wreck – '3009' being nearest the gate! Loaned to the Museum of Transport & Technology in Auckland, where it was restored for display, the aircraft was bought by Ray Hanna who initiated a six-year rebuild with P–40 restoration specialists Pioneer Aero Restorations Ltd based in Auckland.

Flying for the first time in late 1997 the P–40 was shipped to Duxford in England, where it became an important part of the Breitling Fighters display team. Returned to New Zealand in 2004, ownership was eventually transferred to the Old Stick & Rudder Co. and it is now based at Hood Aerodrome in Masterton. The fighter currently wears Chinese Nationalist markings; the civilian registration is ZK–RMH.

No adversary would want to have this aircraft on his tail. Six machine guns and a face
only a mother could love shows that this Kittyhawk is ready to fight.

JOHN LANHAM: P–40 KITTYHAWK PILOT

'Ease out of the loop, careful look round, for goodness sake, don't lose sight of Duxford and Cambridge!'

It's a beautiful morning and I'm flying P–40E ZK–RMH (NZ3009), just northeast of the famous British airfield. Although I gained my RAF 'wings' in the UK, it has been 40 years since I was last pilot in command (PIC) of my own aircraft over this sceptred isle, and I'm taking great care not to get lost. Half an hour of practise aerobatics and a short display over the field – what a perfect way to finish a brief holiday. Some months previously, I had assisted owner Ray Hanna return the aircraft to the New Zealand register before its last display season in UK. 'Next time you are near Duxford, come and fly it', he said. Who could resist such an invitation?

With its lightness in pitch and yaw compared with the longer N models and the type's renowned fast rate of roll, the E model is particularly nice to fly. NZ3009 is one of only three flying ex-RNZAF P–40s left in the world and the only one in New Zealand. The P–40 has been said to be one of the lesser fighters of WWII. Not all would agree, certainly not Ray, who called it 'the most under-rated of all the WWII fighters'. It was also one of the fastest diving fighters, which the RNZAF used to good effect against the more agile Zero, flown by the Japanese and also featuring in this book.

In 1942 the Royal Australian Air Force (RAAF) carried out comparison trials between its older P–40s and the newly acquired Spitfire Mk IXs. The Australians were concerned to prevent the Japanese learning that they had Spitfires and, for security reasons, called them Capstans (after the then popular cigarette). Surely, never in the field of human conflict, was such a beautiful machine given such an unglamorous name. Rather to its surprise, the RAAF concluded that the P–40, at lower altitudes at least, was superior to the Spitfire.

Few would wish to enter that argument and both aircraft have their place in history. In the same way as American and British motor cars do much the same thing but in different ways, the two aircraft have quite different character but both are most rewarding to fly.

STUART GOLDSPINK: P–40 KITTYHAWK PILOT

P–40 Kittyhawk NZ3009 is an E model, which has a slightly shorter fuselage than the later N models and as a result is lighter in pitch. And, with arguably the best ailerons in the business, it's a fine aircraft to display.

The V12 Allison engine is a rugged powerplant, and has half as many moving parts as a Rolls-Royce Merlin. On the air-racing Merlins they use Allison connecting rods for their greater strength over the standard Merlin ones.

It is a beautiful aircraft to fly and very capable of putting on an excellent aerobatic display, including eight-point rolls – not an easy manoeuvre in some aircraft – but the Kittyhawk does it with ease, showing off the splendid aileron response.

This particular aircraft also has a dual set of controls, allowing the pilot the chance to share the great pleasure of flying it with others. Its large tyres also allow it to operate on unpaved surfaces.

Out of a line up of WWII fighters it would be hard to choose a favourite but the P–40 would be very near the top, for sheer aerobatic enjoyment.

CURTISS P–40E KITTYHAWK

LENGTH	31 ft 2 in (9.5 m)
HEIGHT	10 ft 7 in (3.2 m)
WINGSPAN	37 ft 4 in (11.3 m)
ENGINE	Allison V-1710 V12, 1150 hp
MAXIMUM SPEED	378 mph (608 km/h)
RANGE	650 miles (1046 km)
SERVICE CEILING	29,000 ft (8850 m)
ARMAMENT	Six 0.50 calibre M2 Browning machine guns

Stuart Goldspink lands the Kittyhawk at the Classic Fighters Airshow at Omaka. Visibility is restricted over the nose due to the large V12 engine, so care is needed on or close to the ground.

CURTISS
P-40N KITTYHAWK
ZK-CAG (Currawong)

Delivered to the US Army Air Force on 5 May 1943 and one of 848 examples shipped to Australia under the Lend–Lease programme which saw the US supplying Allied countries with war material, this fighter was assigned to the RAAF's No.75 Squadron which was then operating against Japanese forces in Papua New Guinea. On 13 March 1944 the aircraft ran into a ditch while taxiing, but was repaired and returned to operations. Only two months later it was transferred to No. 78 Squadron and was severely damaged during a landing accident at the end of October 1944 which saw it pushed off to the side of the runway and cannibalised for parts. As the war moved on the airframe was forgotten until recovered by Charles Darby in 1974, when the wreck was transported to New Zealand. It wasn't until 1997 that the rebuild to fly got underway, Charles forming a partnership with Garth Hogan of Pioneer Aero Restorations. Completed and finished in original colours by March 2000 the fighter made its debut at Warbirds Over Wanaka a month later, and is now based at Ardmore in South Auckland under the ownership of the Kittyhawk Partnership.

GARTH HOGAN: P-40 KITTYHAWK PILOT

I was forty-eight years old when time and money finally gave me the opportunity to get my Private Pilot Licence (PPL). Cessna 152's seemingly quickly morphed into a Tiger Moth restoration project and then a Russian Yak 52.

When the opportunity arose to work with Charles Darby on the restoration of a P-40N Kittyhawk, it was not to be ignored. At that time, however, the possibility of flying it seemed remote – I was only a 140-hour PPL, with no real Heavy Metal experience.

A conversation with the late Mark Hanna changed that. 'Thirty flying hours in a Tiger Moth, twenty in a Harvard … some from the back seat … and you should be ready for the P–40' was his advice.

The Tiger wasn't finished when the P–40 was completed, so the Tiger-flying element of my 'training' was skipped and, following twenty hours flying in a Harvard, I was sitting in a P–40. What a fantastic machine – it's harder to take off in than a Harvard, but easier to land and an all-round delight to fly. One must always be mindful however of the original purpose of such a machine, and the delights of flying them are always tempered by the memories of those who lost their lives in flying these aircraft in action. As such I consider it an incredible privilege to have had the opportunity to experience the power and aeronautical capabilities of such an aircraft, not to mention a very small insight into what the fighter pilots of WWII experienced.

Two great American V12 fighters are seen here in the skies over Auckland, with the
Kittyhawk leading the Mustang, both very capable fighters.

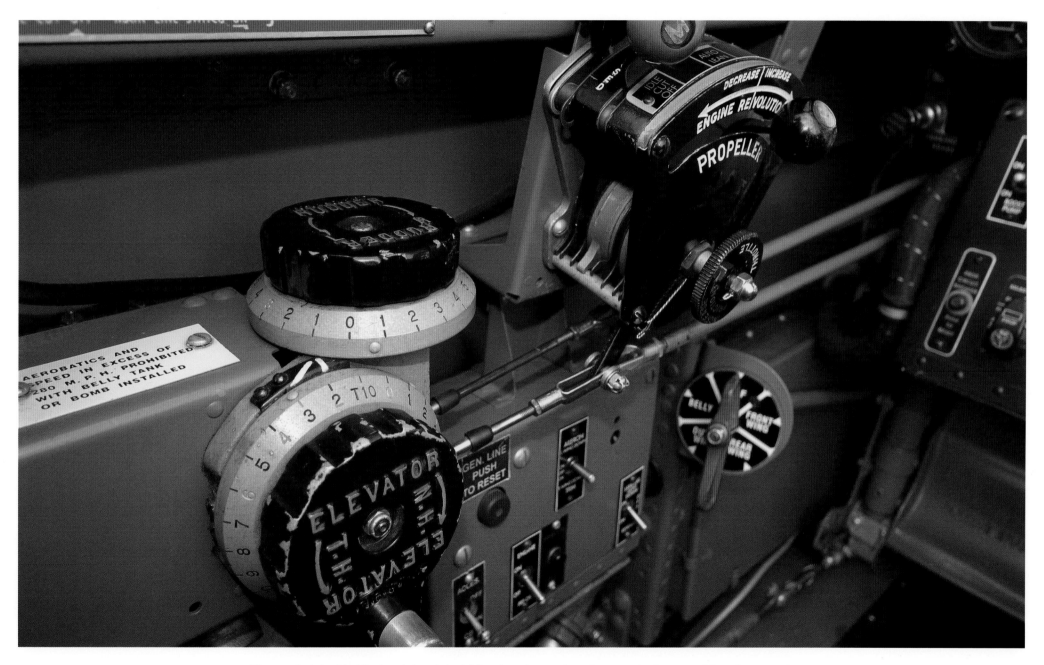

The cockpit in this Kittyhawk is original. The throttle quadrant is towards the top of the photograph with fuel selector below that. Rudder and elevator trim knobs are to the left.

FRANK PARKER: P–40 KITTYHAWK OWNER AND PILOT

When the opportunity to fly a P–40 Kittyhawk became available in 2003 it was not to be missed. My apprenticeship had seen extensive experience in the trainer aircraft the Harvard and in fact I completed my Air Force wings course in this aircraft. On reflection, this training schedule was suited to progression to a World War II fighter.

The P–40 is not a difficult aircraft to fly. At the power settings used it is vastly superior in weight, power and performance to the Harvard; it has similar ergonomic anomalies and with a liquid-cooled engine slightly more complex engine handling. The controls are responsive although the rudder requires attention to maintain balance. The aircraft's forte is its snappy roll rate which makes moves such as Derry turns and half Cubans easy-peasy.

In the airshow circuit, the aircraft is a star in its own right. The pilot's task is simply to 'show' the aircraft and give it personality.

CURTISS P–40N KITTYHAWK

LENGTH	33 ft 6 in (10.20 m)
HEIGHT	12 ft 4 in (3.76 m)
WINGSPAN	37 ft 5 in (11.42 m)
ENGINE	Allison V-1710 V12, 1360 hp
MAXIMUM SPEED	378 mph (609 km/h)
RANGE	750 miles (1200 km)
SERVICE CEILING	38,150 ft (11,630 m)
ARMAMENT	Six 0.50 calibre M2 Browning machine guns

This Kittyhawk can have three panels removed from behind the pilot to make room for a second occupant. It has dual controls making it ideal for training future pilots.

CURTISS
P-40N KITTYHAWK
ZK-VWC (FR350)

Another ex-RAAF fighter which suffered a landing accident in 1944 while operating with No. 78 Squadron, this P–40 bore the legend 'Come in Suckers' on the cowling. Hauled out of the New Guinea jungle by Australian warbird owner and restorer Rob Greinert in 2001 it found its way to Pioneer Aero Restorations Ltd and was eventually sold to Vintage Wings of Canada in 2006. They elected to have Pioneer finish the rebuild and every effort was made to preserve the aircraft as it had been in 1944; one of the few 'upgrades' was the addition of a discreet second seat with a basic set of flight controls in the rear cockpit.

When it came to choosing the paint scheme, it was decided to honour one of Canada's greatest living aces, James Francis 'Stocky' Edwards who flew a similarly marked machine during a yearlong tour of duty with RAF 260 Squadron, Desert Air Force, ending in May 1943, scoring thirteen confirmed kills.

The P–40 flew again in April 2009 – almost exactly 65 years after its last flight. Stocky was able to take control of the fighter for a short time when it was displayed at the Vintage Wings of Canada open day in September of that year – a trip down memory lane if ever there was one!

One other remarkable fact about this aircraft is that it was flown back to Canada in a giant CC–177 Globemaster from the Canadian Air Force. This huge aircraft flew into RNZAF Base at Whenuapai, and swallowed up the Kittyhawk before taking off two hours later with the very precious cargo aboard. Four days later the aircraft was in Canada.

GAVIN TRETHEWEY: P-40 KITTYHAWK PILOT

It was a thrill to be involved with the test flying and some air-to-air photography of the Vintage Wings of Canada P–40 Kittyhawk that had been restored by Pioneer Aero. It was great to be able to show the aircraft to the family of Jim Harvey – the RAAF wartime pilot who crashed the aeroplane on the strip in New Guinea from which it was bulldozed clear and abandoned till recovered many years later.

The Kittyhawk is a bit of a handful to start – it's not the greatest view out, and management after take-off of undercarriage, flap, power and cowl flaps to keep temperatures right keeps your hands busy till you settle down. But it is a lovely aeroplane to fly, and shows itself as a fine stable aeroplane with a great rate of roll – better than the P–51 Mustang or Spitfire – which makes manoeuvring easy. The aeroplane performed all its test requirements well and it was sad to see this beautifully restored aeroplane leave the country, but no doubt we will see more aircraft restored in New Zealand in years to come.

MARTIN HEDLEY: HEAD ENGINEER AT PIONEER AERO RESTORATIONS

To most people the corroded and crash-damaged remains of a Kittyhawk that arrived at the Pioneer hangar would have looked like a pile of scrap. All we saw was the potential that it held.

The fuselage was relatively straightforward to rebuild, especially as there were lots of components that could be made serviceable. The wings were the most time-consuming parts with five spars and various bays for wheels, fuel, guns, and ammunition. One of the challenges in rebuilding the airframe was the undercarriage fairings and the engine cowls. They mostly comprise curves and so figuring out the correct shapes could be very demanding. On the other hand once they were finished it was very rewarding.

With the wings finished and joined it was time to fit them to the fuselage and the fighter was on her own feet again. The next big task was to plumb all the engine systems, jigsaw style, as space was limited.

Then came the big day of the first engine start. I sat in the cockpit and ran through the pre-start checks then pushed the engage button. The Allison is an easy engine to start and this one was no different – she came to life for the first time in nearly sixty-five years. After a few low power runs to check everything, it was time for the high power runs. At 3000 rpm and 52 in.Hg boost the engine was a veritable cacophony and I could feel the power through the airframe. A few adjustments and everything was working as it should. What a buzz.

The first test flight was eagerly anticipated with a mixture of nerves, excitement and relief after all the many hours of work invested in its rebuild.

Interestingly on 25 April 2009, the day of the first post-restoration test flight, the widow, son and two grandsons of Jim Harvey (the pilot when it crashed) were present. It was sixty-five years to the day of the crash, and it was also ANZAC day. Mrs Harvey presented us with an original piece of aircraft skin with the Australian registration number 414 on it and we found the matching piece of skin, with hole, to mate them back together: all very poignant reminders of the kick we get out of restoring these aircraft.

CURTISS P–40N KITTYHAWK	
LENGTH	33 ft 6 in (10.20 m)
HEIGHT	12 ft 4 in (3.76 m)
WINGSPAN	37 ft 5 in (11.42 m)
ENGINE	Allison V-1710 V12, 1360 hp
MAXIMUM SPEED	378 mph (609 km/h)
RANGE	750 miles (1200 km)
SERVICE CEILING	38,150 ft (11,630 m)
ARMAMENT	Six 0.50 calibre M2 Browning machine guns

The photographs opposite show the Kittyhawk being loaded onto a Canadian Air Force CC–177 Globemaster, to be flown back to its new home in Canada.

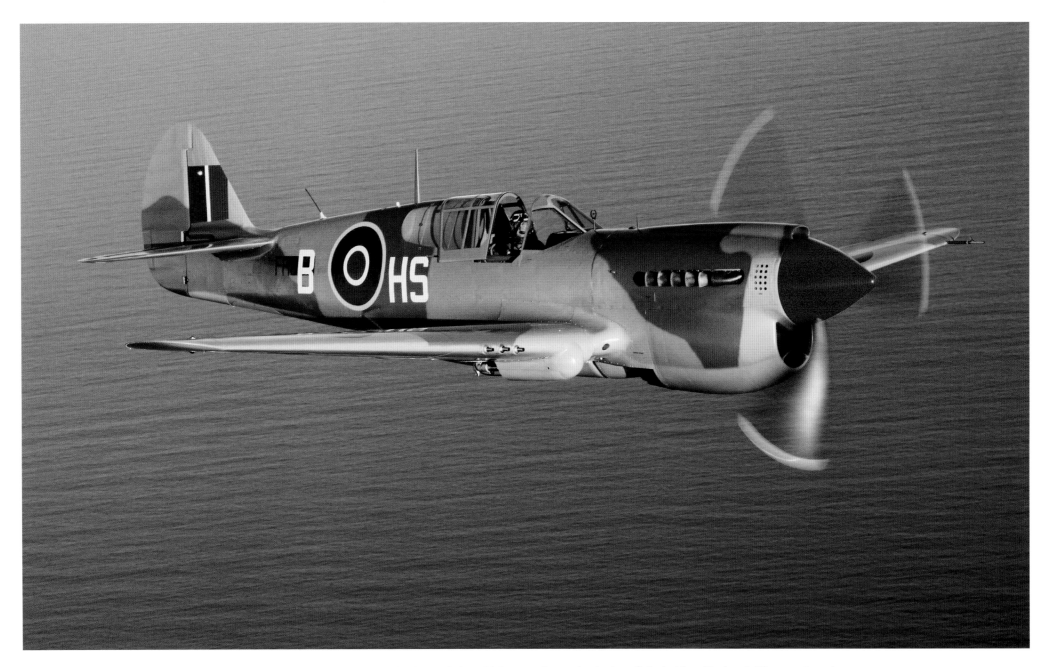

The Kittyhawk is captured during its final test flight which was also to be its last flight in New Zealand. Pioneer Aero have subsequently built several other P–40 Kittyhawks and hopefully we will see more of them flying here in years to come.

CURTISS
P-40C TOMAHAWK
ZK-TWK (AK295)

First flown on 10 April 1941 the P–40C was powered by the 1150 hp Allison V-1710-33 which incorporated an improved fuel system and internally-sealed fuel tanks. However with these improvements came increased weight and as a consequence a drop-off in performance. The Tomahawk IIB was the export version of the P–40C, with additional British armament of four wing-mounted 0.303 inch Browning machine guns, while retaining the American twin nose-mounted 0.50 inch machine guns.

Initially built for the RAF, the British soon discovered the type unsuitable for combat in Europe and many were sent to Russia, which became one of the big users of the Tomahawk. Although their pilots found the aircraft to be a simple machine, it suffered the same problems as all western-designed aircraft did there – the inability to cope with the harsh winters. With some equipment replacement and much improvisation, sorties were able to continue, albeit at a much reduced effectiveness. Pilots found the durability of the airframe, the increased firepower, pilot armour and good range adequate compensation for the lack of manoeuvrability and speed when compared with Soviet types. The Tomahawk however would soon give way to the later P–40 models – they themselves superseded by the preferred Bell 'Cobras' and indigenous Lavochkin models.

The featured aircraft, AK295, was one of the aircraft sent on a ship to Russia from Britain. Arriving there in December 1941 the aircraft served on the Northern Front but had the dubious distinction of being the first combat loss of the type in the European Theatre, shot down on 1 February 1942.

It was eventually recovered from a long forgotten crash site in the former Soviet Union and underwent extensive rebuild in the States before being shipped to New Zealand for the final stages of the rebuild at Avspecs. During early 2011 the aircraft was nearing completion but there was a lot of fit-out work still to be done. With Easter looming, the owner of the Tomahawk, Rod Lewis of Texas, allowed the aircraft to attend the Classic Fighters Omaka airshow and the pressure really came on to meet the deadline as it would be the only time the aircraft would appear at a major New Zealand show. The team worked day and night to get the aircraft ready and it finally took flight on 17 April in the hands of John Lamont. One or two small teething issues were sorted out and the aircraft headed to Omaka one week later.

Afterwards it was flown back to Auckland for disassembly before being packed up into a container and sent to its new owner who will have many years of flying in one of the rarest WWII fighters to be seen anywhere in the world.

The aircraft wears the marking of a Curtiss P–40B Tomahawk flown by American flying ace, Second Lt. George Welch. It had been on station at Pearl Harbour on 7 December 1941 when the airfield was attacked by Japanese forces. George ran to his aircraft and took off to fight the enemy forces. When the battle was over he was credited with four enemy kills – an amazing effort considering the base was attacked by more than 150 Japanese combat aircraft.

The Tomahawk looks factory fresh following restoration. 25,000 hours of blood, sweat and tears were spent on this aircraft and the results are nothing less than stunning.

JOHN LAMONT: CURTISS P–40C TOMAHAWK PILOT

In recent years the P–40 has become a highly sought-after warbird – which is testament not only to its historical significance but also its many fine qualities. The Allison engine is strong, reliable and smoother than a Merlin. It falls short at higher altitudes where engine power declines above about 12,000 ft due to having just a single stage supercharger. The combination of a weighty airframe and reduced performance at altitude meant the P–40 was outclassed by many later production fighters. Its sleek lines and strength made it an excellent diving machine and experienced pilots used this feature to advantage for both defence and attack.

The early model P–40s are a little nose heavy and short coupled and consequently need accurate use of rudder and rudder trim throughout the speed range. This is particularly noticeable on the P–40C Tomahawk. On later models the fin and rudder were moved back 18 inches to improve rudder control and handling. The elevator is quite heavy in contrast with the ailerons which are very responsive and precise.

Once the pilot has become familiar with the control loads and trim requirements the aircraft is an absolute delight to fly and aerobat. The whole package gives a sense of reliability and robustness yet at the same time the aircraft is highly manoeuvrable and viceless.

CURTISS P–40C TOMAHAWK

LENGTH	31 ft 9 in (9.68 m)
HEIGHT	10 ft 7 in (3.23 m)
WINGSPAN	37 ft 4 in (11.38 m)
ENGINE	Allison V-1710-33 V12, 1150 hp
MAXIMUM SPEED	353 mph (565 km/h)
RANGE	730 miles (1175 km)
SERVICE CEILING	29,028 ft (8850 m)
ARMAMENT	Two 0.50 calibre machine guns in the nose, four 0.303 calibre machine guns in the wings

The Tomahawk is powered by an Allison V12 engine. It lacks high altitude performance but down low the engine is a real performer. This freshly overhauled example will see that the Tomahawk stays in the sky where it belongs for many years to come.

WARREN DENHOLM: MANAGING DIRECTOR OF AVSPECS

I never used to rate the Tomahawk very highly. I thought it was the slow, underpowered sibling of the Kittyhawk and after being heavily involved in a handful of 'regular' P–40 restorations I had decided my favourite was the short tail E model. The first time I saw AK295 the fuselage was a gleaming collection of panels and bulkheads held together with literally thousands of Clecos in Tom Wilson's workshop in Georgia. Tom never had eyes for anything other than the Tomahawk. I can understand why now. Without a doubt it is the more attractive and stylish of all the P–40 examples. It stands a little taller with its short tail leg and longer nose. Most wartime pictures of the Tomahawk were taken from the ground and it's not until you see the aircraft from above that the superior cowling lines of this model really become evident . The P–40 line harks heavily back to the earlier hawks with the '75 and the P–36. Basically the first Allison-powered machines were re-engined P–36s. As such the wing and fuselage are an example of true engineering rather than a design brought about by the need to modify something to accommodate a greater number of larger weapons, as in the Kittyhawk.

Easily the rarest example of the P–40 series, restoring the B/C model has posed greater challenges than one would expect. For some, yet to be fully explained, reason, the 'Tomahawk specific' factory drawings are not available. The Smithsonian Institute in Washington DC hold microfilm copies of the majority of US produced aircraft and cover the P–36–40 series with 20 odd rolls of 35 mm microfilm. These drawings have been invaluable to P–40 restorers over the years. In the restoration of the Tomahawk, we were able to find drawings for various parts if they were used in both the P–36 and the P–40, and we were able to find the drawing if the part was used in the B/C model and subsequent models like the E and onwards. If the part was only used in the B/C series then no drawing exists. That has meant that the engine installation and cowlings have had to be re-created from scratch using whatever information could be gleaned from the few original parts we had, and the hundreds of photos we have taken of the largely original example belonging to The Flying Heritage collection based in Seattle. Without the generous access we have been afforded to photograph that aircraft, we would have really struggled to keep AK295 authentic.

The history of this airframe is a little vague, but it appears that it was originally built for the RAF as a Tomahawk IIB. The Red Air Force were being cut to pieces by the Luftwaffe in the early days of 1940 and they desperately needed better aircraft. The Russians purchased a batch of the British Tomahawks and had them shipped direct to Russia from the factory. AK295 holds the dubious reputation as being the first combat loss in the North when it was reportedly shot down on 1 February 1942.

John Lamont breaks from the camera ship. He has probably test flown more P–40s over recent years than anyone else worldwide. A few days after this photo was taken he displayed the aircraft at the Classic Fighters Airshow 2011.

YAKOVLEV
YAK-3
ZK-YYY (Red 12)

The Yak–3 was one of the best Soviet fighters of World War II, particularly at low level where the majority of Eastern Front air battles took place. Designed and built by the Yakovlev Design Bureau, it was robust and easy to maintain, its only Achilles heel being the poor reliability of its Klimov engine and a short range. It was reported that the Luftwaffe issued an order that all fighter squadrons were to avoid combat with any Yak lacking an oil cooler under the nose, unless they were at a height of over 16,400 ft (5000 m) – although how the lack of this feature was able to be distinguished in the heat of battle is hard to imagine.

The type was initially developed in 1941 as a successor to the Yak–1 which had been developed with wooden (and thus relatively heavy) wings, but due to delays the Yak–9 entered service before the Yak–3. A second attempt in 1943 saw the redevelopment and weight reduction of the wings which markedly increased the speed the fighter was capable of to 407 mph (655 km/h). The new Yak–3 began operating in 1944 with the Soviet Air Force, and also equipped the famous volunteer French 'Normandie-Niemen' Squadron who accredited themselves so well that Stalin allowed them to return to France with their aircraft at war's end. When production ceased in mid-1946, the total number built had reached 4848.

Surprisingly, very few original Yak–3s survive and it wasn't until the early 1990s that there was any hope of seeing a representative of this important combat aircraft gracing the skies. Given the importance of the type it was a glaring omission on the airshow circuit. The only possible solutions were to convert the post-war two-seat Yak–11 trainer or reopen the original production lines and resume construction. The latter was accomplished for a period of time, with 'new' Yak–3 and –9 production undertaken at the original factory in Orenburg in southern Russia; however this came to an end during 2004.

In the meantime several collectors opted to reverse engineer the relatively common Yak–11 trainer, which had the same wings as the Yak–3, but significant fuselage construction differences – notably smaller tubing dimensions. As there would be little chance of obtaining an original Klimov engine because few survived the war, power would be provided by an American Allison V12 engine.

The aircraft featured here is based on a Yak–11 trainer and was converted to fighter configuration in Russia for Ray and Mark Hanna of the Old Flying Machine Company in Duxford before coming to Pioneer Aero Restorations Ltd in Auckland. There it was completed and painted in the colours of Russian fighter pilot Lt. S. W. Nosow of the 150 Guard Fighter Regiment/13 Air Division in 1945. First flown in April 2005, the Yak is now owned by Arthur Dovey in Wanaka and he is enjoying flying this very capable fighter.

The Yak–3 is a very lightweight fighter with a powerful engine. During WWII, German pilots were instructed to avoid combat with a Yak–3 if possible, such was the reputation of this fighter.

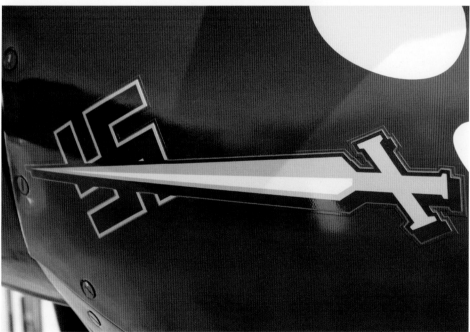

ARTHUR DOVEY: YAK–3 OWNER AND PILOT

The Yak–3 is one of the most pleasant aircraft I have flown, and has a similar performance to the de Havilland Vampire jet. Trim changes over the whole speed range are minimal, producing low stick forces; coupled with an impressive power to weight ratio, this produced a fighter that was without doubt most impressive in a dogfight. The only drawback is the lack of aerodynamic warning when pulling g at low speed. The fighter will flick easily and I understand this was a manoeuvre used by Russian pilots in combat. I have not tried this tumbling manoeuvre but according to Colonel Stephen Barber of the Commemorative Air Force, 'it will certainly get your attention'. A measure of the Yak–3's performance is a true airspeed of 270 knots at 9000 feet with 2100 rpm and 27 inches of boost. The wide track undercarriage gives a stable ground roll on both take-off and landing, the only difficulty being the poor visibility caused by the long nose during landing, necessitating a curved approach to very late finals. All aerobatics are easily flown with less than climb power producing an aircraft which is just a delight to fly.

YAKOVLEV YAK–3

LENGTH	27 ft 10 in (8.5 m)
HEIGHT	7 ft 9 in (2.36 m)
WINGSPAN	30 ft 2 in (9.2 m)
ENGINE	Allison V-1710 V12, 1480 hp
MAXIMUM SPEED	407 mph (655 km)
RANGE	405 miles (650 km)
SERVICE CEILING	35,000 ft (10,675 m)
ARMAMENT	One 20 mm cannon and two 12.7 mm Berezin UBS machine guns

Arthur Dovey takes flight at the Classic Fighters Airshow 2007. This aircraft
is a real crowd favourite and is admired wherever it goes.

The small stars by the cockpit were applied to aircraft to show how many aerial victories were credited to individual pilots. It was hard enough to become an ace with five victories let alone shoot down fifteen!

NORTH AMERICAN
P-51D MUSTANG
ZK-TAF (NZ2415)

The P–51 Mustang came about following a request from the British for an American fighter to help equip the hard-pressed Royal Air Force, whose supply of Curtiss P–40s was at capacity. Designed, built and flown in the remarkably short time of just 178 days, the prototype first flew on 26 October 1940. The P–51 incorporated some new aeronautical design features, notably the 'laminar flow' wing. Laminar flow is the smooth, uninterrupted flow of air over an aircraft and an important factor in flight. The wings designed for the P–51 Mustang were designed so as to have less drag at high speeds. It also had a new radiator design which used exiting hot air to provide thrust to assist forward momentum. This concept is known as the Meredith effect, named after its designer Frederick Meredith.

Despite these features, however, high-altitude performance was found to be substandard, as the Allison engine was primarily a low-altitude power plant. Nevertheless a few dozen fighters, dubbed 'Mustang' by the British, were delivered to the RAF and made their combat debut on 10 May 1942. With their long range and excellent low-altitude performance, they were employed effectively for tactical reconnaissance and ground-attack duties over the English Channel, but were of limited value as fighters due to their poor performance above 15,000 ft (4572 m), where much of the European air war was fought.

There was however no doubt about the potential of the airframe itself, and a stroke of genius by the Commander of the RAF's Air Fighting Development Unit which was testing the aircraft, saw Ronnie Harker from Rolls-Royce's Flight Test establishment invited to fly it. Rolls-Royce engineers rapidly realised that equipping the Mustang with a Merlin 61 engine – which had a two-speed two-stage supercharger – would substantially improve performance. Their findings were sent back to the US where the necessary changes were made: the airframes were strengthened to accommodate the extra power; the ventral radiator was deepened; and the carburettor intake was moved from above the nose to below to accommodate the Merlin updraft induction system. The rest, as they say, is history!

Although not introduced in quantity until the spring of 1944, the P–51D became the model produced in the greatest quantities, with 7954 being completed. Powered by the Packard Merlin V–1650–7 1590 hp, two-staged supercharged 12 cylinder V engine, its huge range meant it could escort bombers to the farthest reaches of the Reich. By the end of the war in Europe, P–51s claimed some 4950 aircraft shot down (about half of all United States Army Air Force's claims in the European Theatre), the most claimed by any Allied fighter in air-to-air combat, and 4131 destroyed on the ground against the loss of around 2520 aircraft.

Post-war, the 'Cadillac of the Sky' saw action in Korea and was operated by at least twenty-five countries around the world for more than thirty-five years, the Dominican Republic operating them as late as 1984.

Shortly before the end of the war, New Zealand ordered 320 Mustangs to replace the Corsairs, but by war's end only thirty had been delivered and the remainder of the order was cancelled. Eventually allocated to Territorial Air Force units around the country, where they served in a training role until 1955, they were thereafter offered for sale and sadly the majority were scrapped in 1958.

Our featured aircraft, ZK–TAF, is an ex-USAAF and Royal Canadian Air Force fighter that wears the scheme of one of the ex-RNZAF P–51s – NZ2415 flown by No. 3 Canterbury Territorial Air Force squadron.

This aircraft arrived in New Zealand during the early 1980s and was the first World War II period fighter to fly actively in New Zealand for many years. Its arrival reignited the passion for so many people, including a new generation who had never seen or heard a fighter like the Mustang. It was displayed for many years in the capable hands of Trevor Bland and is now owned and flown by Graham Bethell, who continues flying this iconic fighter in the same enthusiastic fashion. He can be seen flying his Mustang at most air shows around New Zealand and his displays are very popular. Graham served as a fighter pilot with 75 Squadron RNZAF and flew Skyhawks for several years. Being able to fly a beautiful Mustang today is one of his greatest passions. Graham refers to the P–51D as 'my sixty-five-year-old girlfriend and isn't she beautiful'. What a great tribute!

The Mustang prepares to taxi out with a very lucky passenger in the back seat. The view from the cockpit is superb due to the one piece blown canopy. This aircraft has been based in New Zealand since the 1980s and is owned and flown by Graham Bethell.

GRAHAM BETHELL: P–51D MUSTANG OWNER AND PILOT

The P–51D Mustang is considered by many to be the world's best ever fighter, so it is a real privilege to own and operate this classic aircraft. In World War II the P–51D with its six 0.50 calibre machine guns would definitely have been the fighter pilots' 'weapon of choice' as it could fly higher, faster and further than just about anything else.

Airshow crowds love the sight and sound of the Mustang with its 27 litre, supercharged V12 Rolls-Royce (Packard) Merlin at high power, and I enjoy displaying it for them. It is hard work though, as the P–51D was designed as a long-range bomber escort, so keeping this high energy machine nicely in front of the crowd is quite a challenge.

As is the case with many high performance aircraft of its era, she can be rather difficult to handle on take-off and landing, which is a pity really because those events happen on every flight! Once airborne and up to speed, however, the Mustang is a pilot's delight – well harmonised and agile, with power to spare.

I hope that my love affair with this beautiful lady continues for many years to come.

NORTH AMERICAN P–51D MUSTANG

LENGTH	32 ft 3 in (9.83 m)
HEIGHT	13 ft 4 in (4.08 m)
WINGSPAN	37 ft (11.28 m)
ENGINE	Packard V-1650-7 Merlin V12, 1590 hp
MAXIMUM SPEED	437 mph (703 km/h)
RANGE	2300 miles (3701 km) with long range tanks
SERVICE CEILING	41,900 ft (12,780 m)
ARMAMENT	Six 0.50 calibre M2 Browning machine guns

Graham Bethell brings the Mustang in close to the Hercules camera ship.

Brett Emeny forms up alongside the Mustang in a de Havilland Vampire jet. The Vampire was a bit late to see service in WWII but it did signal an end to piston-powered fighters.

NORTH AMERICAN
P-51D MUSTANG
ZK-SAS (Dove of Peace)

Strangely enough American war pilot Colonel Glenn E. Duncan's choice of nose art did not please the powers that be. The insignia of a swooping skeleton firing guns and the legend 'Angel of Death' first appeared on his P–47 Thunderbolt, but although the insignia was to remain, the name was changed to 'Dove of Peace' – the irony of which is self evident. One time commander of the 353rd Fighter Group, Duncan ended the war with 19.5 kills and passed away on July 14, 1998. However he and his P–51 are remembered every time P–51D-20-NT Mustang, 44–13016, leaves the runway at Wanaka airfield in the South Island.

Although far from the dangerous skies where its namesake flew, this particular machine is quite close to its original home of Australia. Manufactured in late 1944, the aircraft was shipped to Australia and allocated to the Royal Australian Air Force (RAAF) as A68–674, but was never assigned to a Squadron. Post-war the fuselage was sold to a farmer in Benalla, Victoria and later to Pearce Dunn, who ran an aviation museum at Mildura. Eventually arriving in the US for restoration, it was finished in a spurious RAAF scheme. Robert Borrius-Broek of Jet Flights Wanaka Ltd bought the aircraft in September 2004 and two months later it was shipped to Pioneer Aero Restorations Ltd in Auckland, where it was reassembled and tested before flying to its new home on 23 February 1995. Robert currently displays the fighter at air shows over the spectacular Wanaka scenery and being one of the lowest-timed airframes of today's flying Mustangs he is likely to do so for some time to come!

ROBERT BORRIUS-BROEK: P-51D MUSTANG OWNER AND PILOT

At times Mustang enthusiasts ask me, 'What's it like inside the Mustang cockpit during flight?' The best way to describe it is that just like any other warbird, it is the purest form of unadulterated aviating: you're using your hands and feet all the time, while exposed to indescribable noise, vibration, engine and oil smells; without proper hearing protection, you'd risk permanent hearing loss very quickly – but what a blast! With no previous warbird experience, my instructor advised me that when I was proficient in taking off and landing the Harvard from the back seat, I should be ready to try my hands on the Mustang. What great advice that was; the transition was straightforward. Referred to as the 'Cadillac of the Sky', the Mustang's handling both on the ground and during flight is a delight. Lower the nose from cruise attitude and she just takes off, wanting to go faster and faster.

Due to her sixty-six-year-old age however, we have reduced the maximum speed from 438 knots to 380 knots to protect the airframe. Fly at speeds of over 350 knots and the flight controls become quite stiff. Using the elevator trim wheel makes life a little easier. Nothing gives me more pleasure than to share a ride in our Mustang with a fellow P–51 aficionado and for many of those who have joined me it has been a very emotional experience. At times I have to pinch myself when cruising through the Southern Alps near our Wanaka home base, as I watch the mountains turn pink during a summer's evening flight and think to myself, how very privileged I am to be the keeper of the keys of this magnificent machine until the next generation takes over. It really doesn't get any better than this.

Modern jet trainer versus WWII fighter; the Mustang still looks great flying beside the L–39 Albatros as they form up behind the Hercules camera ship at Warbirds Over Wanaka 2008.

NORTH AMERICAN P–51D MUSTANG

LENGTH	32 ft 3 in (9.83 m)
HEIGHT	13 ft 4 in (4.08 m)
WINGSPAN	37 ft (11.28 m)
ENGINE	Packard V-1650-7 Merlin V12, 1590 hp
MAXIMUM SPEED	437 mph (703 km/h)
RANGE	2300 miles (3701 km) with long range tanks
SERVICE CEILING	41,900 ft (12,780 m)
ARMAMENT	Six 0.50 calibre M2 Browning machine guns

This Mustang is kept in pristine condition. It has a full set of dual controls and operates from Wanaka airfield where it can be heard reverberating through the mountains.

The Mustang takes off from Mandeville airfield following a fly-in held there. The passenger in the back is obviously enjoying himself as the Mustang blasts skywards.

This period of the take-off is a busy one for the pilot. The landing gear can be seen retracting, while the flaps will retract as soon as cruise power is selected for the trip back to Wanaka.

OPPOSITE PAGE Lake Wanaka comes into view as the Mustang climbs out for the photo flight at over 3000 ft.

LAVOCHKIN
La-9
ZK-LIX (White 28)

This particular Soviet fighter aircraft didn't fly until 1946, but because its design began in 1945, and was based on some famous Lavochkin-built fighter aircraft, we have featured it in this book.

Developed from the wartime mixed wood and metal La–7, the all-metal La–9 was actually a new aircraft, even though it bore a family resemblance to its predecessors. The lighter aircraft retained the 1850 hp ASh–82FN radial engine, had an increased fuel capacity and armament of four cannons mounted on the nose. The fighter first flew in June 1946 and deliveries commenced in early 1947, with supplies going to East Germany, China and North Korea. It was allocated the name 'Fritz' by NATO.

As with the last of the Allied piston fighters such as the Hawker Sea Fury, Grumman Bearcat and Corsair, the La–9 found itself deployed mostly in the ground-attack role during action with the North Korean Air Force, which had two regiments of the fighter operational in the Korean War. But, despite its impressive performance, and a maximum speed of 690 km/h (430 mph), the aircraft could not match the latest US jet fighters.

The type had eventually faded from front-line service by 1960 – the piston era well and truly consigned to the history books. By that time 1630 single-seaters and 265 two-seaters had been built, but once again little thought was given to preserving examples. Only five are known to have survived, and of those only one is airworthy.

Ray Hanna of the Old Flying Machine Company spent many years negotiating with an aeronautical museum in Beijing to buy it and finally swapped it for a Harrier jet. It arrived at Duxford in May 1996 and was dispatched to Pioneer Aero Restorations in Auckland for restoration. The airframe was substantially complete by 2002, by which time Ray had entered into a partnership with Pioneer's Garth Hogan over the aircraft. However the engine rebuild in the Czech Republic held the project up markedly and a first flight did not take place until March 2003. Shipped back to the Old Flying Machine Company, its original Chinese Air Force colours were replaced with the Soviet Red Star as the Chinese objected to the use of their insignia without permission.

After a short display season the fighter returned to New Zealand and made an impressive appearance at Warbirds Over Wanaka in 2006. It would do so again for one final time at the 2010 show, where some of these air-to-air photos were taken. From the author's point of view, the test flight before Warbirds Over Wanaka 2010 was a thrilling sight. The aircraft hadn't flown for four years and on the eve of the show John Lamont roared down the runway and into the air. He slowed the aircraft to check the engine and systems, but from the ground he appeared to be really moving through the sky and after the checks were completed he flew a very nice low-level display that left me with goosebumps, such is the charisma of these fighters. John once said, 'It's like holding a tiger by the tail and doing your best to keep it under control'.

Following the show the La–9 flew to Auckland where it was packed up and shipped to a new owner in the US. It will be enjoyed there by a new generation who have never seen a Lavochkin La–9. Thanks to Ray Hanna's passion we have been able to see the world's only airworthy La–9 show off its potential.

John Lamont takes the La–9 vertical at Warbirds Over Wanaka 2010. John says 'Its like holding a tiger by the tail and doing your best to keep it under control'.

JOHN LAMONT: La–9 PILOT

This aircraft together with the La–11 represents the last of the Lavochkin series of high-performance piston engine fighters. The design is simple but sophisticated and features a laminar flow wing mated to a clean fuselage. At normal operating weight of 3300 kg, the powerful and sturdy 1850 hp ASh–82FN engine delivers startling performance. Armament is provided by four NS–23S 23 mm cannons mounted in front of the pilot and firing through the propeller. All four firing together would be something to experience!

The La–9 is without doubt the most exciting aircraft I have flown and is an aircraft with serious attitude. It can be a real handful on the ground with its small rudder and lack of tail wheel steering, but considerable care and correct technique ensure successful departures and arrivals. The flying characteristics are similar to early generation jets – well harmonised and light control forces combined with small trim changes throughout the speed range. Dial up the power and speed and the aircraft develops an incredible throbbing sensation through the airframe. Haul it into some high speed, high-g aerobatics and watch the vapour trails off the wingtips. Wicked!

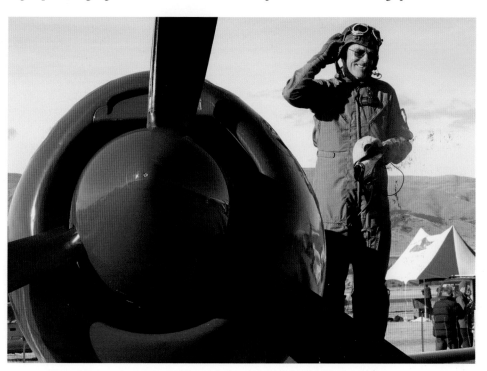

KEITH SKILLING: La–9 PILOT

Like an earlier Russian fighter, the Polikarpov I–16, the La–9 is very exciting to fly. This aeroplane gave me more 'moments' than I have experienced during my entire warbird flying. The same is probably true for John. We have both been off the runway landing it, and on one memorable occasion I went off the runway both on take-off and landing! I departed Duxford on my way to Le Bourget for the Paris Air Show and accidentally gave it too much power, too soon. Instantly I went thirty degrees left off the runway and just made it over the boundary fence. Thirty-five minutes later I was still shaking as I landed in Paris and broke several runway lights having suffered brake failure. The La–9 sure is an exciting ride.

The Lavochkin was Ray Hanna's pride and joy. His first flight was at Duxford and on landing he did a beautiful 360-degree ground loop and continued the landing roll straight ahead. He taxied in as if nothing had happened, but with a huge grin on his face. He said it was both faster and more manoeuvrable than the Sea Fury or Bearcat.

LAVOCHKIN La–9	
LENGTH	28 ft 4 in (8.47 m)
HEIGHT	11 ft 8 in 3.56 m)
WINGSPAN	32 ft 2 in (9.80 m)
ENGINE	Shetsov ASh–82FN, 14 cylinder radial, 1850 hp
MAXIMUM SPEED	430 mph (690 km/h)
RANGE	750 miles (1200 km)
SERVICE CEILING	35,433 ft (10,800 m)
ARMAMENT	Four 23 mm cannons

Although the La–9 is now based in the United States, we were very lucky to see it fly here in New Zealand, as it is the only one of its type flying in the world.

The large 1850 hp radial engine dominates most of the forward section of the fuselage. The two large cannons running along the top of the engine are obvious, with two more on the other side. The bullets pass between the propeller blades.

John Lamont takes off from Omaka bound for Auckland, the last time we would see the La–9 in the South Island.
Once in Auckland it was packed up and shipped to the United States for new owner Jerry Yagen.